That's What *Love* Looks Like

A JOURNEY OF FAITH, REDEMPTION, & UNCONDITIONAL LOVE

GRACELY

WESTBOW
PRESS®
A DIVISION OF THOMAS NELSON
& ZONDERVAN

This book is a work of non-fiction. Unless otherwise noted, the author
and the publisher make no explicit guarantees as to the accuracy of
the information contained in this book and in some cases, names of
people and places have been altered to protect their privacy.

WestBow Press books may be ordered through booksellers or by contacting:

WestBow Press
A Division of Thomas Nelson & Zondervan
1663 Liberty Drive
Bloomington, IN 47403
www.westbowpress.com
844-714-3454

Because of the dynamic nature of the Internet, any web addresses or
links contained in this book may have changed since publication and
may no longer be valid. The views expressed in this work are solely those
of the author and do not necessarily reflect the views of the publisher,
and the publisher hereby disclaims any responsibility for them.

The Four Loves by CS Lewis © copyright 1960 CS Lewis Pte Ltd
The Case for Christianity by CS Lewis © copyright 1943 CS Lewis Pte Ltd
Extracts used with permission

ISBN: 979-8-3850-1908-3 (sc)
ISBN: 979-8-3850-1907-6 (e)

Library of Congress Control Number: 2024903146

Print information available on the last page.

WestBow Press rev. date: 8/20/2024

Contents

Embracing the Power of Love

No other topic in the world has been written about more, whether in literature, song, or theater. It's a topic often discussed as something being searched for or lost. We are talking about **L O V E**. When love is absent, there is hate, envy, strife, joylessness, covetousness, and everything ugly.

Someone once said that three things are lasting. They are faith, hope, and love; though all three are essential, love is the greatest.[1] I don't believe having hope or faith without love is possible. Love, or the lack of it, explains or defines the motive behind the things we say and do. Love is the most potent force in the world and has the power to change everything.

Because love is a topic covered in zillions of books, I can quickly talk myself out of writing this (my first published) work. And if it wasn't something I was convinced I was supposed to do, I wouldn't write it. The idea of writing a book was planted within me before 2007 and then when I went through cancer treatment that same year, the topic was deposited in my heart. Somewhere between 2011 and 2012, a stranger who handed me a receipt at a car dealership where I was getting repairs done, out of the blue, asked me the following question. Ever think about writing a book?

Soon afterward, the title of this book was the very words I spoke to a widow when she asked me why I was painting the inside of her house at no charge.

Now more than ten years later, it is time to finish this book. I had an earlier version of this book. It got scrapped two years into writing, and the format ended up very different than originally planned. You will find my personal life stories in an attempt to tie these stories to the truths I wish to share. It is a work that is definitely more open and raw than I had initially planned. This book takes you on a journey of what love looks like, both in experiencing and receiving love as well as giving love away.

It's 2022, and I came across a note that contained the last words that my Mom wrote to me after she had had a stroke and lost her ability to communicate verbally. She wrote, "Get it done". I knew she was referring to this book. It sounds like a great reason to get this project finished.

Seeds of Love

Childhood Memories, Teenage Years, & Formative Experiences

CHAPTER 1

My Childhood Friend

I had an extraordinary friend when I was five or six years old. I would talk to this friend with slight confusion as life appeared to be different than what others were telling me how life should be. Though I had nothing traumatic going on with three brothers, both parents and grandparents living with us, I saw a disconnect. I remember telling my friend that there had to be more to life, and I was hungry to have "the more."

As most of us experience as we get older, we tend to lose touch with childhood friends. And that was my experience with this particular friend. As I got older, his involvement with our family seemed to lessen. Though he never wanted to be distant from my family and me, I started to do my own thing without much thought of including him in my daily activities.

At 14 years old, I discovered that a junior high schoolmate and I had something in common. Gail knew my childhood friend I had lost touch with, and she invited me to start spending time with our mutual acquaintance.

My relationship with my childhood friend was rekindled. The more time we spent together, the more I realized I couldn't live without him. Everywhere I went, I wanted my friend to go with me. He became my best-est friend ever! We had become inseparable, and that friendship grew stronger and stronger until....

CHAPTER 2

Life is Not Going as Planned

I can honestly say I was in love with being loved by another, but I don't know that the two of us ever grasped what true love of another looked like. I was married at age 24. My husband was a big dreamer, and our worlds growing up were very different. I'm not saying my life was better than his, but it was different. We both had been raised by parents who loved us very much, but nothing else between us was the same. One of us had very goal-oriented folks with an upper-middle-class background where there wasn't a lack of nice, material things, but not much physical affection was displayed. Birthdays weren't a big deal as more candles were to be added to a cake, and the other holidays weren't much different than any other day. The other of us didn't have much in the way of finances, but expressing love between family members was never in question, especially with all the hugging. Celebrations of one another with lots of food, family, and friends gathering were common. They never lacked reasons to come together for feasts and fun.

After almost 15 years of marriage and at age 39, my

spirit was crushed, and things came to the lowest low. The marriage was full of deception, lies, no contributions into the household finances from my spouse, signs of infidelity, illegal activity that threatened my financial and physical well-being, and lots of disappointment. It all came to a head when over $10,000.00 was put on my credit card without my knowledge until the bank called that they were closing the account due to non-payment. This led to a divorce I didn't want. It was best after years of on-again-off-again counseling sessions and many broken promises. The counseling sessions ended up being a time of me unloading verbally and going home feeling better only with empty promises, plenty of lies, and no behavioral changes in my husband's life.

I didn't realize how much my identity was wrapped up in being a wife. When the marriage ended, I had lost who I was apart from being a wife. I didn't know what to do with myself, for I felt like a total failure. Things weren't supposed to end this way! I wasn't familiar with divorce or the damage it would bring to those involved.

My special friend never left me, but instead of allowing my best friend to help me through this challenging time when the divorce happened, I started looking for validation in all the wrong places. Jesus was my best friend, but I shut Him out when I entered an adulterous relationship. I would do things my way.

CHAPTER 3

It Truly is a Slow Fade!

It was a rough time in my life, the late 1990s. I had just gone through a traumatic life incident and felt very much out of place. Divorce will do that to you. Although I was around others most of my waking hours, I felt like a spare wheel. Now that my spouse was no longer a part of my life, I forgot my identity as a chosen, adopted child of God.

It was a progressive thing that started with the flattery of a single guy on the church's worship team who gave me much-needed attention while my heart was crumbling with hurt and a massive sense of failure. I'm sure I didn't just wake up one morning and decide to take the reins of my life out of God's hands and drive it in a different direction altogether. It was more like what one song says is a "slow fade." But in no time, that slow fade had become a fast-moving dive into emptiness and severe loneliness.

These are the lyrics of *Casting Crowns' song titled Slow Fade:*

It's a slow fade when you give yourself away
It's a slow fade when black and white are turned to gray
And thoughts invade, choices are made, a price will be paid
When you give yourself away
People never crumble in a day
It's a slow fade, it's a slow fade

Instead of running to God for continued direction, strength, and comfort, I looked for the answers in another who was just as broken as I was. Not only was I experiencing the loss of a marriage relationship, but my new lifestyle, filled with wrong choices, separated me from the One that had been my source of life, peace, and joy for decades. I found myself not able to pray, and I was miserable. Though His love for me never wavered, I had shut Him out, and it was no longer a two-way relationship with Him.

I decided to take the control of my life out of His hands and do all the navigating of daily living on my own. He didn't stop me from making my decisions, and He won't in the future.

Even though I was making a mess of my life, *That's What Love Looks Like. #FREE-WILL!*

CHAPTER 4

From the Frying Pan to the Furnace

After about three months of doing things my way, I decided I didn't want to stay in the pig slop anymore. Or at least that's what I thought at the time. I missed my time with the Lord. I broke off the relationship I was in that got me rolling down the wrong path, and I turned to Jesus, who was waiting for me to cry out for help in the mess I had made.

I had asked God to forgive me for failing Him and getting involved in an unholy relationship, but I was still spiritually bankrupt and not mentally in a good place. I hadn't repented. Repentance is more than asking for forgiveness. It's having a change of heart that results in lifestyle changes that desire to please God versus satisfy self. After my divorce and about a month after breaking up with guy #1, a neighbor introduced me to guy #2, and we went out on a blind date. The first date should have caused me to run the other way; however, I saw financial security in him and admiration towards me. Financial security wasn't something I had experienced in my first marriage, and this guy showed interest in me! The morning after our blind date, I went to his house which led to moving in with him. Deep down in my heart, I knew this relationship wasn't right. But I had two unidentifiable blinders over my eyes, and within a year, I was married to my blind date.

Husband #2 had a stable family life, and our upbringings were similar. We had met each others' families within a month or two of our first date, and everyone seemed to like one another. He had a Christian upbringing and even had a degree in Pastoral Studies; he had at one time planned on being a pastor. He was funny, had a great military career, and a job, and was financially responsible. We were attracted to one another and had lots in common.

Things were great for the first few years of our marriage. We went to church regularly, had great careers, went on vacations several times a year, and didn't have a care in the world. To the natural eye, we looked like we had it "all together." However, things were going south at a steady pace. By year seven, things were definitely not right, but I couldn't put my finger on what the problem was.

All the time we were together, I thought he just had an overactive sex drive. I began to believe that my life and the things in the bedroom were normal. Close to year six of marriage, I remember him telling me he needed to have sex seven times a day. I was traveling during the week and would come home on the weekends to have no rest. Besides wanting me to satisfy him sexually, he always had a house project waiting for me to work on when I came home for a day or two between weekday work trips, regardless of how tired I was.

For seven years, we could never talk about improving our relationship as husband and wife or how to strengthen our relationship with God. I would try to start conversations with the hopes that we would discuss things in the Bible. I remember taking a book out one evening centered on a Biblical marriage and starting to share something that I thought was really great. He became defensive and argumentative. He replied sharply, making sure I understood that this kind of conversation would never be brought up again.

I would continue to read my Bible and fellowship with other believers. Before my divorce from husband #1, my life was all about sharing with others about the God who loves us unconditionally. I would play the piano and sing with others publicly in places of worship. All that had come to a stop. I was trying to please my husband #2 without much success. I felt like a robot going through the motions of life. I had literally "lost my song" and didn't know how to get it back.

I was baffled as to why things weren't improving between my husband and me and why my relationship with God hadn't been restored. I would feel worse after attending a church service. Worshiping Him was difficult and a very painful experience for me. This was especially true in a corporate setting. It constantly reminded me of my close relationship with the Lord before I failed Him. I missed that closeness with my God and couldn't see a way to return to the spiritual state of my pre-divorce days. Thankfully, I continued to seek God for answers, even though I turned up empty-hearted and disappointed for eight years. He was and has always been the answer to all of my life's challenges and questions. I was doing things that would foster a relationship with Him, but I felt God Himself had left the building. And then it happened!!

CHAPTER 5

I'm Just a Dirty, Useless Candle!

One Sunday, we decided to go to a different church than the one we attended for the past seven years. At the end of the church service, an announcement was made that there would be a ladies retreat in six days. I thought, "Why go when you are just going to be disappointed again?!?" But I had a sliver of hope that things could be different this time and I would have a breakthrough in my relationship with God, so I decided to attend. I didn't know it then, but I was soon going to find out I had unforgiveness towards myself, and I would finally see *what love looks like!*

So I'm at this ladies retreat where I don't know anyone. The theme was tied to an acronym SPARC. I'll never forget that Saturday morning for as long as I live. The guest speaker had two candles. One candle had never been lit, and it was perfect. It was tall and slender. It hadn't been burned, and it was lovely. The second candle was dingy, dirty, used, and scarred, with visible markings. I could truly relate to that second candle. I thought to myself, "That's me! I'm like that dirty, ugly candle!" I had convinced myself that God could never use me again for all my mistakes and wrong choices.

And then, the guest speaker broke down the word SPARC. I listened intently as she mentioned that the S letter stood for shame. I have no idea what scripture she shared or what else she said about shame. I checked that off my mental list as not a problem for me, and thought it must be for someone else! Then, she mentioned that the letter P was for pride. Suddenly, I realized these were the two unidentifiable blinders that had been a part of me for eight years. I had worn a cloak of shame all these years and I couldn't see it because of pride. These two blinders had distorted everything around me and had robbed me of my true identity in Christ.

I cried through the rest of the talk as the rest of the letters in the word SPARC were explained. The letter A stood for anger and boy, was I angry and frustrated to the hilt. And there was an R for regret. If I could have relived my last seven to eight years, I would have. But as we all know, there's no going back. And last, there was the letter C, which represented condemnation. There were heaps of that. I was deceived and convinced that God could never use me again. Ever! I was a divorcee who had messed up with one of my church worship team members. And have I mentioned that husband #2 was addicted to porn and an alcoholic? Yup!

I had made a mess of things, but now God was washing over me with His love, and the tears kept coming. For the first time in eight years, I had assurance that God loved me! And not only could God use me again, but He would take pleasure in seeing that very thing unfold.

I went home that day a different person, with a new

hope and excitement that God could take my life and make something useful out of it. I sat down at my piano and sang the song His Strength is Perfect for the first time in years. But this time, I was singing it from deep down inside of me with confidence that what I was singing was 100% true. God had set me free from all the shame and the pride that had me bound for so long. The cloak of shame had been traded in for a garment of praise and His righteousness. Now, I could worship my God without the chains of shame, pride, anger, regret, and condemnation!

Now *That's What Love Looks Like.* #FREEDOM!

CHAPTER 6

The Devil is mad!

God began doing great things in my life, and I could feel God's presence again. Months have passed since the ladies retreat. I'm praying that my husband will experience a closer relationship with God. I wanted that for him so we could serve others and love our God as a couple.

Here are parts of what I wrote in a book titled Words of Promise, authored by several of us at St. John's United Methodist Church. At the time of this write up, I knew the scripture referenced would be part of this book.

Back to the Basics:

It's May 3, 2007, six months after the ladies retreat, and time stood still. My doctor had just told me that what he saw looked cancerous. I immediately gave the news to my parents and my husband, sharing it factually as if I were stating tomorrow's weather report. I comforted them and told them I was okay. God knows where I am and what's happening, and I am in His hands.

About an hour or two after my diagnosis, all my formality gave way, and the flood waters came. I told God

13

I didn't want to suffer much pain and didn't want to die. I enjoyed my life here on this earth and wanted to reap the benefits of my almost 30 years in healthcare. I cried until I couldn't cry anymore. That day was one of the most emotionally taxing days of my life. I ended the day by going to bed early, hoping things would look brighter the next morning.

Since the day of that life-changing news, the emotions have been more even-keeled. I thought about the possibility of my life ending at a younger-than-usual age, which made me ask, "What's next? What do I do now?" And it seemed the answer came in the simplest form, something I already knew but needed as a gentle reminder.

There was a time when Jesus told a lawyer what the greatest commandment of the law was[2] and then Jesus said, "If you love me, you will keep my commandments."[3] So obeying Him is one way He (and we) know we love Him. I believe what I've heard author/speaker Kevin Zadai say, that "obedience is God's love language." And in my personal times of struggling to obey Him, it's my relationship with Him that is somehow being hindered. It's usually me not spending enough time with Him, just like in any other friendship when together time is lacking. A disconnect happens.

God reminds us that he prefers obedience over offering Him the best sacrifice.[4] Our best sacrifice isn't as good as just doing what He asks us to do. Finally, my questions took me to a place where Jesus tells us that He gives us the *power* to *become* the sons of God.[5] Becoming what God wants us to be is a process, and we don't "become" without His help or in our limited strength. Wow! What a wonderful promise we can rely on.

For everyone who is born into this world, there is one appointment that we are going to have to show up for. We don't like to talk about it, but our time on this earth will one day end. Whether we have an illness that could point to a more predictable date of death, whether we are part of what we call the rapture of the saints, or whether the timing of our death is an unknown, it matters not. I realized the frailness and unpredictability of life and that my diagnosis didn't change a thing. I needed to do what I always knew to do. Simply know what He wants me to do, become what I'm created to be, and out of a love relationship between us just do what He asks me to do. He promises to provide me with the means of making this possible.

Prayer: Dear Lord, thank you for reminding me of what's most important when put in the proper perspective. And I pray to you for Your peace. Amen!

Shortly after I wrote the above for the Words of Promise book, all havoc broke loose in my home, and I realized that what I thought was expected in the bedroom was abuse. I had never been around abusive behavior but was now in for many more surprises. The sexual abuse continued, but the verbal abuse that began was much worse. The devil—whose name is Satan and is God's chief enemy— no longer had a grip on my life, and he wasn't happy about that. Neither was my husband.

During my chemo and radiation treatment, my husband was struggling. Before we met, he had lost his mom to a slow and painful cancer-related death. I don't think he had ever really dealt with it, and now he was looking at another cancer diagnosis. Though he came to the hospital every other day when I was doing inpatient treatments for 16 days, little if any, compassion or concern was shown toward me. When I was home during the treatment months, he still needed to be sexually satisfied, so even though I was in extreme pain and had very little energy, that was an expectation of his that didn't stop.

After three months of medical leave, I returned to work. I had also started teaching classes at church, was part of the worship team, and was more hands-on with local church ministry. I was spiritually and physically growing stronger each day. However, the verbal abuse grew in intensity and severity. I was accused of being a pathological liar and being unfaithful. One night, my husband told me I could move out if I wanted to continue to teach Bible lessons. This was followed by him hugging me and, in tears, asking me never to leave him.

I remember the last Christmas we spent together in 2010. As we drove up to my parent's place to celebrate, he started shouting at me uncontrollably with false accusations. I was confused. And each time there was a disagreement, which had become more routine with us, I would try to reason with him. Things didn't make sense, and nothing I said or did mattered.

Afterward, it dawned on me that for the past ten years, everything that gave me pleasure—my friends, my family, teaching the Word of God, sharing myself with others— was something that Satan wanted to strip from me. I was blinded by this reality until the Lord delivered me from shame and pride, but now my eyes were wide open. The devil was trying to destroy me while using my husband to do the dirty work. My husband didn't want to share me with anyone or anything that gave me joy.

His behavior was so unpredictable. One minute, my husband would tell me I was the best thing that ever happened to him, and the next day, he expressed great hatred towards me. He questioned everything I said while not believing a word I spoke. On top of my confusion, I didn't know what to do or how things would improve.

This is definitely *Not What Love Looks Like.* #PERPLEXED!

CHAPTER 7

Three Strikes, I'm Out!?

Cancer treatment was over, and the New Year of 2011 arrived. I went back to work as a traveling Healthcare IT professional, and things were great as far as everyone around me was concerned. I was getting rave reviews from my clients, people were asking for me specifically to fill their contract requests, and bonuses were continuing to be an added benefit on top of an excellent salary. However, I had been assigned a project for nine months that I disliked, and things at home could not have been worse. I felt that there was something else I needed to do with my life, and I returned to the prayer of my childhood: "There has to be more God, and I want it!" I had been praying this for the past couple of years, but I was getting more serious with my request.

The phone rang in February 2011, and I was hit with a job layoff. After the initial shock wore off in about 15 minutes, there were three directives I felt God spoke into my heart. He told me to be STILL, KNOW who He is, and WAIT on Him. I had plenty of time to "know" but those other two four letter words were challenging. Yes, you could drop one L, and stil would still be still! And to wait on or to wait for something? Very few of us enjoy playing the wait game.

I shared with my husband I felt impressed to hold off on getting another job. He wasn't happy with this decision, and without an interview, I was offered a pretty lucrative job, making more money with many more perks doing what I had been doing the prior nine months which I disliked. My passion was teaching, but the job offer involved more consulting work and less classroom time.

I asked the new company to give me a couple of weeks to think about it since I was getting ready to go on a pre-layoff, planned vacation. I KNEW with every fiber in my being I wasn't supposed to take the job, and I was hoping my husband would feel the same way after two weeks, but that didn't happen.

I felt like I was in a vise. There was no reasoning with him on this matter. To keep peace in the home and to try to pacify my husband, I accepted the job. I thought I would put God on hold for two years. This was the minimum time I had to work for the new company without paying back any training costs. After all, I was determined to make it work and what is two years anyway?!?

Strike #1 was my disobedience in taking a job when God told me specifically not to. I remember the feeling I had when I faxed the acceptance for this job. It was as if something inside of me died. It was nothing short of awful. I reasoned that I would take the job for a few years, things would get better at home, and then I could quit the job. Though my intentions were good, my priorities were messed up big time!

God had made it clear what He wanted me to do, and I blatantly disobeyed Him. God doesn't keep us from things because He doesn't want us to have a good time or to control us. Instead, He gives us instructions and guides us because He knows what's in our future and wants the best for us. If we'll only listen! The freedom I felt in Christ for the past four years since the ladies retreat seemed to have instantly slipped through my fingers. When a person intentionally disobeys their heavenly Father, it doesn't cancel out their kinship with Him, but it opens the door for God's enemy to attack. I had a target on my back, and Satan took little time to take advantage of the situation.

Other than my cancer in 2011, I had always been healthy. For all the years in healthcare, I was either sharing the air with sick people in hospital hallways or breathing air with others flying 30,000 feet in a closed-in, aluminum tube and yet I rarely got sick. What happened next was not coincidental. God was trying to get my attention, but I was oblivious to any warning signals sent my way.

Strike #2 was on my health just a few days after accepting the job I wasn't supposed to take. I had been on a bike trail that we frequented dozens of times without incident. But this time, I got bit by what we assumed was a spider. I was scheduled to leave for the new job's employee orientation on Monday morning. I was in the hospital Saturday night with a bad case of cellulitis from the spider bite. I called my new boss, and we rescheduled for a later date.

Strike #3 came shortly afterward. I was scheduled for training within two or three weeks after my spider bite. A couple of days before I was to leave the second time for the job I wasn't supposed to accept, I ended up in the hospital again. This time, it was with an 89% blockage on the front artery of the wall of my heart, aka the widow maker. My doctor told me I should have died in ten days when I first had the symptoms since, during that time, I had gone on a 25-mile bike ride, cleaned an RV, and swam 50+ laps daily with continual discomfort that I ignored. I ended up with a stent and making a second phone call to my new boss saying I was in the hospital.....again! You would have thought that by now, I would have gotten the hint that God was giving me a way out to walk away from this new job. But being the strong-willed person I was, I got out of the hospital and got my training in and on to my new employee orientation. I was on a roll but rolling in the wrong direction!!

Is this What Love Looks Like? #PATIENCE!

CHAPTER 8

Leaving

One late evening, I came in from my new job of two weeks, and a terrible argument broke out between my husband and me. And for the first time in my life, I saw in his eyes the spirit of murder. My husband's life was engulfed and controlled by the one who hated us both. And with me walking in disobedience, with the new employment, the devil would have loved to have taken us both out. The following day, with hubby at the golf course, I was pretty ill from the arguing and the abuse that had ensued into the early morning hours. My head was splitting with a migraine, for I had only slept about eight hours in the past three days. God spoke to me to get up, pack, and leave.

Jesus says that we are His sheep, He knows us, and as our shepherd, we hear His voice as we follow Him.[6] I had not even considered leaving the marriage of 11 years, but I had no doubt it was God's voice and not just some thought of my own. Leaving home was too close to being divorced, which was the last thing I wanted, but I told God that if He made me well, I would get up and do as He spoke. Instantly, all signs of the migraine left, and I packed.

I had enough hotel points to stay in a hotel for a week at no cost, so I decided to do just that. I stopped by my folks' house to tell them that I was leaving home but without giving them any details of the problems that we were having. I protected my husband's reputation because I believed God would help us and things would improve. I didn't want my folks to have bad feelings towards him if our marriage mended. I intended to get my 40 hours of work in for the week and spend the rest of my day praying. And I believed God would help me. God was my only hope and the solution to our problems.

After getting to the hotel, I headed to the bookstore looking for answers. I discovered that many problems were connected to my husband's addiction to pornography and his attempt to cover up his sorrow and bondage with alcohol. I purchased two books once this understanding was clear to me. One was Beth Moore's book, *Get Out of That Pit*, and another was *Pure Eyes* by Craig Gross & Steven Luff. These books helped me examine my life and our marriage in the light of God's love for us.

Even in this part of my journey, God never failed me. Sometimes, I am a slow learner.

He was trying to show me then *What Love Looked Like.* *#GRACE!*

CHAPTER 9

Enrolling in the School of Surrender

It was clear to me my husband believed with all of his being that all the problems we were having were all mine, and this wasn't going to be something that would be resolved in a week. Though my husband was not to blame for all of our problems, things wouldn't change if alcohol and porn were to remain in the mix of our relationship.

It was April 2011. I had been hit with a layoff in a job that served me well for many years, my Dad had been diagnosed with and failing quickly with Alzheimer's, I had left home not knowing whether my marriage was salvageable. All these losses on top of accepting a job I had no business taking on, happened within days of one another and I was broken.

After a week of being away from home and running out of free hotel nights, I needed a place to stay for an undetermined amount of time. Six months prior, I had visited a friend, a church pastor in the panhandle of Florida. As she gave me a tour of this quiet, small, quaint town, I loved what I saw, and I remember saying these exact words: "This is paradise, and I would love to live here, but it will never happen." Six months later, this was the very place I headed for, and I never left.

Based on my husband's horrific phone calls, texts, and emails, it was apparent he wasn't interested in reconciliation. I spent weeks crying out to God to save our marriage and to help me become more like Him.

About a month into my new job, I attended church on Sunday morning, and by Sunday night, I was distraught. My worship was shut down because of my disobedience. My God looks for people who will worship Him in Spirit and in Truth. When a person is living in outright disobedience, there is no truth in that life. I was living a lie, and if things were going to get better, there were changes I had to make.

After the evening church service, I tried to finish my 40-hour workweek but couldn't concentrate. I remember flying out of the bedroom into the living room of my pastor/ friend's house and weeping uncontrollably as I told her all that had happened. From the spider bite to the heart stent, I knew I had to quit the job. The morning couldn't get here fast enough so I could make the phone call.

I made the call, apologizing to my boss, and the weight of the world I was carrying on my shoulders lifted. There were many unknowns that I would face; however, I took comfort in knowing that I was better off with uncertainties in trusting a God that looked after His own versus the alternative of trying to navigate with my limited understanding void of God's involvement.

I also lived in a town with people I loved being around. I love the promise that tells us if we delight ourselves in Him,

He gives us the desires of our hearts.[7] The very location I thought would never be the place I'd call home had become my own. Though it was one of the most challenging times of my life, it was the most rewarding in spiritual growth. I had entered into the life-long school of total surrender. More lessons were forthcoming in learning about *what His love looked like.*

It's 2020, and I feel God is speaking to my heart about the three businesses I've been building since 2013. It's like He's having me evaluate how I spend my time more and more. I believe this is because of the day and age we are living in. He's soon to return, and many people don't know Him.

These businesses, as well as playing computer games, in and of themselves are not harmful or sinful. They were just taking up lots of my time. With much hard work, the businesses had been profitable and beneficial for those with whom I've had the privilege of partnering. Even so, He wants me to increase our time together, and have more ministry time with others. Sometimes, we have to say no to some things to say yes to other things that we're called to do. And after experiencing consequences of disobedience, my response this time would be different!

So, Father God, I say, "Yes to You, and continue to show me *What Love Looks Like.*" #OBEDIENCE!

Trials and Triumphs

Facing Heartbreak, Overcoming Adversity, & Difficult Relationship Lessons

CHAPTER 10

Santa Comes Early

It was nearing the 2011 holiday season, and I'd been away from home for seven months. I was unsure how the marital story would end; my pastor friend was out of town and I was alone with no family nearby. I didn't know exactly where I would live long-term. I was jobless. I was concerned about my Dad's health. I'm still married, but my marriage was all but dead. Though the past few days had been fantastic as I delighted in the goodness of God, I was still experiencing sorrow and grieving the many losses in my life. My heart was wounded, and I was hurting. But, I was intentionally seeking my heavenly Father. I was asking Him to kill me so I could live. Kill all SELFish desires so I can become the person He meant for me to become.

Thanksgiving Day was around the corner and I'd had two or three days of fantastic encounters in prayer, Bible reading, praise, and worship time. It was a mountain-top experience spiritually, and I thought I'd head to a nearby beach to enjoy the sound of the waves and take in a sunset.

As I was getting ready to leave the beach, a gentleman

was looking at my Volkswagen Beetle, and he struck up a conversation. My spiritual antennas didn't take long to sound off an alarm as the flattery started rolling off this guy's lips. That's how I got into trouble the first time after my divorce from husband #1, and I didn't want to rewind and replay that scene again with a different leading man.

I believe demons schemed what I'm about to describe, and God allowed me to be tested. Why wouldn't He test me if God our Father would allow a famous man named Job and His only son, Jesus, to be tested? Just a thought!

Here's how planned out this entrapment was, with the hopes of derailing and destroying me. The guy with the flattering speech was from one of my favorite towns in Michigan, had several real estate businesses, had a home on the beach in my new hometown, and his place in Michigan had horses. He was a widower, and his wife whom he lost to cancer, was a pianist (sound familiar?) and he wanted to exchange phone numbers. He thought I was beautiful! Actually, he called me classy, but who cares? I enjoy horseback riding and saw financial stability and a potential life partner. Oh, did I mention to you that his nickname was Claus? Yup! I couldn't make this up if I tried. The "perfect" person to come along to tempt me and get me off the path of growing stronger spiritually and emotionally had a nickname of Santa!

I didn't give him my number, but I took his phone number without promising I'd call him. I returned to my temporary dwelling place and struggled as I tried to read my Bible and close out my evening. My conscience was gnawing at me, and I felt convicted about keeping Claus' phone number. So I got up from where I was sitting, deleted the phone number from the phone I was currently using, and put it into an old phone that was no longer in service. I was still holding on to the thought that if I changed my mind, I'd have the number to fall back on. You know, have a Plan B. Thankfully, seconds later, I did the right thing and deleted the name and phone number from my phone, which was the end of Claus! I mentioned earlier in this book that sometimes I'm slow, but with some practice, I'm getting better at spotting traps that will lead to disaster. I'm committed to being a lifetime student in the School of Surrender and living a life of obedience to the Lord. When we exercise trust and faith in the One who is faithful and trustworthy, life is much more pleasant!

Job said some profound things during his time of testing. This is one of those statements: "Yet He knows the way that I take; when he has tested me, I will come forth as gold."[8] From that day on, I have told myself that there is "NO PLAN B!" I've come too far, gone through too much crud, to compromise and not be 100% sold out to living my life to glorify my heavenly Father. I chose to make Him my plan A to Z. And I like gold!

That's What Love Looks Like. #COMPLETE!

CHAPTER 11

Say What, God?

So I'm going back and forth between my friend's house in the Florida panhandle and my folks' place every couple of weeks, making a round trip of 13 hours of driving. I'm tired, and my marriage is still in a holding pattern. There are no positive indications of restoration, but I keep hoping. Hoping my husband will want to be free of his addictions and that we can both make the necessary changes to work things out.

I'm laying in bed, praying and crying out to God to help me when, to my surprise, His response was, "File for a divorce." God hates divorce. I remind Him of this hatred, and I'm struggling to understand why I would need to be the one to file for such final legal action.

Some might think this sounds "off" and that God wouldn't tell someone to divorce their spouse. It sounded off to me and appeared contrary to God's character. In writing this, I'm reminded in the Bible, God told a prophet to marry a prostitute. This is just one example where we have many preconceived ideas of what God will and will not say or do.

If we could figure Him out, He wouldn't be God. That's part of the excitement of living for Him and why reading the Bible and discerning the voice you hear as a thought or a gut feeling is vital. He promises He will lead those who trust Him, so we need to listen to His voice.

The Bible says to "work out your own salvation with fear and trembling."[9] I certainly don't want anyone reading this to think that divorce is something to take lightly or that what I'm saying gives you or anyone else the advice or encouragement to divorce your spouse. What may be the right thing to do in one person's situation may not be the best choice for another person, even in a similar scenario.

You often can't explain what you believe God is speaking to you to do in words that others will understand. Still, there's a sense of peace outside of our personal understanding[10] and we know without a doubt that we are hearing our Father's voice. We not only recognize His voice as sheep would know the voice of their shepherd, but we will know when a voice speaking to us is not His.[11]

Years ago, I learned something neat about sheep. There can be multiple flocks grazing together in a field but when their shepherd calls for them, only those that belong to that specific shepherd will respond to his voice. This voice recognition is based on the sheep's prior experiences and interactions with the shepherd. There's a sense of trust and familiarity that the sheep have because of the tender care and time that is given to them by the shepherd. They know the shepherd's voice from all other sounds in their environment. And that's the way it is in having a relationship with our Father. We will know His voice apart from other distracting voices that come from the world, from our friends and family, from our self-will, or from Satan, the enemy of our souls.

Back to my conversation with God and after reminding Him that He hates divorce. I asked Him how it could be that He was telling me to divorce my husband and why. I heard God clearly say to me in my heart, and I quote, "There are some things I hate more than divorce!" This conversation between Him and me took place during the weekend, and I intended to obey Him and file the papers on Monday morning.

When I went to file for divorce, I discovered that my husband had beaten me to it. Opinions are like noses in that everyone has one, but I'm convinced that God wanted to see if I was willing to obey Him and do what He asked of me. I said, "I will." Obedience. Even when it hurts, you do what's best because you love the One in charge of your life. You want to please Him. And obedience is honored and rewarded by Him.

That's What Love Looks Like. #TENACITY!

CHAPTER 12

Knock, Knock! Anybody Home?

With all that was going on simultaneously in my life, I must admit that it was the start of a deeper walk with God that I would describe as priceless. I was sad, full of rejection and hurt, but at the same time, I was being wooed by the One who loved me the most. I was seeking Him daily for hours at a time. Literally on my face, my main focus was for Him to reveal and change anything in my life that didn't resemble His likeness. During these months, many times, I just groaned. Words wouldn't come as I was experiencing so much brokenness, but one thing was for sure. I wanted God to be in the center of who I was, to be THE One I desired more than anything or anyone. Just like that little child knowing there was more to life, I wanted to experience it in Him and from Him. He was very present in applying healing to me.

With the divorce filed, I needed to find a place to live. The town I was in was where I wanted to stay, but outside of that, I didn't know where I would end up. I prayerfully started looking at houses, and I put an offer on two short-sale properties, with one place being a small house outside of the city limits with birds singing, a large backyard, and on the inter-coastal waterway with a private dock for my kayak. The other property was a duplex in the town center surrounded by great neighbors, and very spacious with lots of storage space. It was like a picture-perfect setting where a white picket fence would fit great with the landscape. I made an offer on both properties simultaneously but wanted the duplex. I had checked out the duplex several times with the Realtor and even went by myself a couple of times to pray, thinking this would be the perfect neighborhood in which to live. I bought paint swatches for the place. I mentally could see myself living there. God was leading me, but not as I suspected.

It was a Monday morning, and as I did most mornings, I started my day by reading the Bible and worshiping the Lord. I was excited to meet the Realtor at the duplex with my paint swatches at noon. But in the middle of my worship time, I suddenly heard Him speak challenging words to my heart. We had a conversation, and I remember it like it happened yesterday.

God: "Lay the duplex down."

I thought God was joking. I mean, here I was, a career woman of 33 years (which has nothing to do with anything....ha, ha), depending on a friend for my housing, and on top of everything else, I was attending a church where I was leading the music where World War III was breaking out because we weren't singing the songs that have been sung for the past 50 years. There are too many "hers" being sung and not enough hymns. In other words, too many contemporary songs are being sung instead of traditional hymnals. I would physically get sick before each church service due to the contention over the music selection. Still, I knew I was assigned to stay there. The carpet beneath me that had been soaked with tears for months was not even my own, and God was positioning me for another loss!? I felt pretty sorry for myself and tired of not having a place I could call my own.

Me: "I mean, really, God. I've lost a job, I'm losing my Dad and my marriage, and you want me to give up something I WANT! I really, really want this duplex, God."

God: "Give it to me; lay it down."

After this conversation went on for 15-30 minutes with me screaming and kicking like a spoiled brat, here's the next thing I heard.

God: "You can have the duplex if that's what you want, but if you want me more, lay it down."

Wow. God had my attention, and I needed to decide what to do. Exhausted from the fight of my will against God's......

Me: "OK, it's yours, God. I ask that you take the desire for the duplex away from me."

I had another thirty minutes after my tantrum ended before meeting the Realtor. I quickly drove to the property and sat quietly in my car. Once my Realtor joined me, I told her I needed to do the walk-through myself, so I went upstairs and left her downstairs. I looked the place over thoroughly and realized I had NO DESIRE for the place. I mean NONE whatsoever! It was GONE!

When I returned downstairs, I had tears streaming down my face, and with relief and a peace that was amazing to me, I told her I didn't want the place. I'm sure Peggy was thinking, "What'chu talkin' about, Willis!" For those that aren't familiar with the sitcom of the late 70s to mid-80s titled Different Strokes with child actors Gary Coleman and Will Smith, see the YouTube clip https://www.youtube.com/watch?v=bJd1RktjYTU and that sums up the sense of perplexity the Realtor had when I explained to her I no longer wanted this property and to cancel my offer on this place as well as the property on the water. God told me to do something different than my upbringing would have advised me.

God's best is always better. Part of loving Him is doing things that are difficult for us but give Him pleasure and opportunity to work in and through us. God used what the enemy meant for evil and turned it around for His good regarding the church music. The most verbal, disgruntled people became close friends, and we extended forgiveness to one another.

I love this writing of a famous physician: "What I'm trying to do here is get you to relax, not be so preoccupied with *getting* so you can respond to God's *giving*. People who don't know God and the way He works fuss over these things, but you know both God and how he works. Steep yourself in God-reality, God-initiative, God-provisions. You'll find all your everyday human concerns will be met. Don't be afraid of missing out. You're my dearest friends! The Father wants to give you the very kingdom itself."[12]

I'm also reminded that the kingdom of God consists of righteousness, peace, and joy.[13] And who doesn't want more of these things? Sign me up!

God had changed my heart and replaced my desires with His. It was truly miraculous. This is not the first time this has happened, and as you continue reading, you will see it is definitely not the last time!

That's What Love Looks Like. #TRANSFORMATION!

CHAPTER 13

The Dog Choir
Answers the Door

I shared with my Realtor briefly what had taken place earlier that morning and that God had something better planned for me. Even though I didn't want to admit it, God wanted me to be in a specific part of town, rent, and not own.

To rent a place was a significant leap of faith for me. This directive to rent sounded like nonsense to me. I was taught that rent was an expense that lines someone else's pockets with nothing to show for it in the long run while the money put towards purchasing a house is an investment you can call your own. At the time of this decision to rent, I had been a homeowner for about 30 years. But God's ways are not like man's ways,[14] and we cannot continue making decisions based on our earthly wisdom and knowledge. If we want to walk out a life according to God's unique plan, it will most likely be different than what we expect.

The past twenty years had not been so kind to my newly found neighborhood, with more crippling legislation placed on the seafood industry and the closing of a paper mill, one of the town's largest employers. One section of town seems to have suffered the most. Poverty was more evident there, and that's where God wanted me to rent. I called this section of town the Dog Choir Neighborhood because there were just as many dogs as there were people, and they would not just bark. They would sing at all hours of the day and night. Sometimes in harmony, sometimes in unison, but primarily off-key!

One of the neighborhood Dads was nicknamed Bubba, and his dog's name was Bubba. Sometimes, this family didn't have running water, and many yards nearby looked like a dump. I had befriended a couple from out of state who had a house in this neighborhood. It wasn't for sale, and it wasn't for rent, but it was next door to Bubba. And guess where God wanted me? Yup, you guessed it. Next door to Bubba and Bubba! I had already started looking at houses for rent, and the pickings were slim to none. Since I was living on my savings, the lower the rent, the better.

Not only did the out-of-state couple agree to rent the property to me, it was on the low end of my budget, and the floors were all tile. It's been my preference to not have carpet. This seems a little thing but significant when added to the fact that EVERY room in the house was painted a different color, and each room's color matched ALL of my home décor to a tee! So what's my point?? There is no coincidence with God; He loves giving gifts to those that love Him. [15]

It took some time to get used to the idea of living in a section of town where the lifestyles and lack were foreign to me. I have never thought myself better than other people who are different from me, but I didn't have family or friends who dealt with poverty. And the house I rented was less than half the living space I was used to, and the closets were so small I had to make one of the teeny bedrooms my closet. Poor me. I was so deprived! I'm being sarcastic here, but at the time, it felt like another loss I had to deal with. How wrong I was!

In my new rental house, I continued to seek God and look to Him for guidance. I no longer desired to purchase a house, and that desire was still gone at the time of this writing. I had obeyed the Lord in moving to this specific part of town. Even though the God's spirit was living inside me and He is the source of joy, I lacked both joy and contentment.

After several months, I remember one morning just getting up, and joy had arrived in my soul. Contentment hit me like a ton of bricks, and I started singing and dancing in the hallway of my new little house. Well, it wasn't mine, but you know what I mean.

I finally realized the joy of being in the center of His will and grew in my love for Him. I still smile today at how He has orchestrated all of this for His honor and glory.

I could see *what His Love Looked Like! #PROVISION!*

CHAPTER 14

I Didn't Sign Up for This or Did I?

When I was getting moved into the "dog choir" house, the landlord wanted me to finish up the bathroom they had just tiled, so I picked the color mauve to paint the walls. I lost a grip of the paint as I gave it one last shake before opening it, and out of the gallon can, the mauve paint spilled on the newly grouted tile. I was excited about moving in and having my own place again, so I didn't let the spill steal my joy. I called a neighbor who came to my rescue after I asked her to come quick with a bunch of rags. I ended up salvaging enough of the paint to not have one drop left at the finish of the job. Yay!

Immediately after that paint fiasco, the cold water pipe in the bathroom closet started leaking. I continued to sing and thank God for the place He provided for me and called a plumber. The plumber came and went, but moments later, the hot water line next to the one that had just been repaired started leaking. The water line was fixed after it took the plumber a couple of hours to return with the parts needed to complete the job. All was still going well with my attitude until I went outside.

I needed to clean the paint pan and brushes, so I went outside to the water hose. The spigot had a lock on it, and I couldn't get the lock off to turn the water on. At that moment, I lost my cool. You could say the water hose broke the camel's back. I raised my fist to the sky and told God, "I didn't sign up for this!" All I could think was if my spouse had just wanted to work things out, I wouldn't be in this mess with a rental property six and a half hours away from my folks, dealing with all these mishaps by myself! I was ticked off and decided to share my feelings with a pastor's wife, Myrna.

I told my friend Myrna about all that happened and my response to it all, and just as sweetly as she could, she said, "Oh, yes! You signed up for this!" She told me that the moment I decided to obey God and follow Him, I signed up for this and more, but things would be okay.

In those moments, my neighbors didn't see a reflection of His love, but since that day of "losing it" at the water faucet, God has shown me over and over again who He is.

What does Love Look Like? #FAITHFULNESS!

CHAPTER 15

Close Call

I have to go back a few years, but I didn't want to leave this or the next chapter out because it speaks volumes about the character of my God.

The year was 1998, and I dreamed I was in the house of my youth and standing near the back door. On the other side of the door, there was an ugly spirit. The enemy of God was trying to get into the house to spiritually kill my three brothers. In the dream, I was pulling on the doorknob and refusing to let the enemy enter.

When I awoke, I felt a strong urge to go to all my brothers and just encourage them to take inventory of where they were in their relationship with the Lord.

I remember going to each one of them. The one that was most challenging to visit was my oldest brother, Wayne. There was a nine-year difference in our age, and we had never been close or even talked to each other much. He had been in and out of jail most of his adult life until the last few years before my dream.

Wayne was brilliant. He could take things apart and put

them back together better than they were initially made. His boss told me later that he could go into a room where an electrical job was done and identify whether or not Wayne had been assigned to the job. He could spot Wayne's work apart from everyone else's because it was far above average. The only problem is Wayne didn't like being told what to do, and for most of his years, he used his intelligence to accomplish the wrong things.

He got arrested once for breaking into a church and then another time for stealing electricity from the power company. After this arrest, someone in the executive offices of the power company called our Dad, asking where Wayne learned how to do what he did because some of the best in the field wouldn't have been able to do what he did without getting electrocuted. Up to that time of his life, Wayne hadn't gotten any formal training as an electrician, but everything he did was done meticulously! Even in acts of crime!

I decided to give Wayne a Bible, so off I went to my folks' place where he was staying. I tearfully started the conversation with an apology. I told him I was sorry for not being the sister I should have been, and I wanted him to know that even though we were like strangers, I loved him. I handed him the Bible and encouraged him to read it, telling Him that Jesus died for him so that he could know Him and experience His love personally.

I didn't stay long. I said what I wanted to say. I just remember Wayne being attentive to my words and accepting my apology. I left hoping that something I said would make a difference in his life. And maybe it would also open doors for us to get to know one another better.

Wayne was starting to get his life together, and working towards getting his electrician's license. Within two weeks after we spoke, a brain aneurysm burst, and Wayne landed face down in a ditch, brain-dead while he was working alongside his boss.

Shortly after our talk, Wayne told our parents how much he loved them and hugged them. I found out later that Wayne often talked highly about our family to others, surprising us siblings and parents because he wasn't one to show affection towards any of us. That wasn't the grumpy Wayne we knew. This was especially the case with our parents, whom he hadn't told he loved since childhood. This massive behavior change must have resulted from a heart transformation that only God could perform.

Before I wrap this chapter up, I have to share a funny story. While Wayne was on life-support machines and we were praying for God to heal him, my parents and I went back to their place. Wayne loved to smoke pot, and Mom found quite a large stash in his dresser drawers. She handed me several baggies full of the stuff, told me to get rid of them, and spoke these famous words I heard a couple of times from Mom: "And don't say anything to Dad!"

Well, what am I supposed to do with it?!? We decided I'd flush it down the toilet, so off I went. Midway through the flushing, I suddenly realized that if God healed my brother, I was in big trouble because Wayne wouldn't be happy with me getting rid of his pot! God healed Wayne, but not on this side of heaven, so I was safe! Whew!

I'm glad God speaks to His children in various ways. And for some of us, He has to get our attention while sleeping. If I had had a passing thought of going to visit my brothers, I probably would have dismissed it and nothing of any importance would have happened. The dream was so dramatic and seemed so real that I felt a significant danger, which caused me to take action. I believe it made an eternal difference in at least one of my brother's lives, and we will have eternity to get better acquainted with one another.

I'm looking forward to that!

That's What Love Looks Like. #INTERVENTION!

CHAPTER 16

Nothing Salvageable

Wayne was born on Thanksgiving Day, and we decided to take him off life support machines on Christmas morning, 1998. Wayne was an organ donor, so we met with the organ harvesting team and learned of the hundreds of people who could benefit from our family's loss.

The harvesting company had a lengthy process, which included asking us dozens of questions about Wayne's medical history, lifestyle, and habits. In this time of loss, it was encouraging to learn that Wayne's death could bring life to many others needing medical intervention. And with him being just 48 years old without any known health issues, we thought things looked really promising for the harvesting team. They told us that the following week, they would call my folks and let them know how many beneficiary recipients received life-giving parts of Wayne.

Just days before Christmas Day, my folks and I went to the funeral home, and when my Dad went to get something out of Wayne's wallet, a business card fell out of the wallet. I picked it up. I'm glad I didn't hand the card back to Dad.

It was a calling card for sexual favors and prices with my brother's contact info. Other than being totally surprised about what I saw, I didn't give it another thought. It wasn't anything to focus on then, and I just slipped it into my pocket and forgot about it. This was one thing I definitely wasn't going to tell Dad! Or Mom, for that matter.

Christmas morning came, and my parents and I said goodbye to Wayne. The organ harvesting company representative was outside Wayne's door. They expressed their condolences, and we headed to the elevators to go home. Suddenly, the calling card came to mind, and I told my folks I wanted another minute and would join them in the lobby shortly.

I'm sure they thought I had wanted additional private time in Wayne's room before leaving; however, I needed to say something to the organ-harvesting employee. Because of the calling card that dropped out of my brother's wallet, there was a possibility that Wayne's organs wouldn't be able to be shared. So, I just asked the rep to do me a favor. If, for any reason, they found something wrong with Wayne that would be bad news for my folks to hear, they would simply tell my folks that there had been an infection in his bloodstream that must have entered his system through the trachea tube. This way, if Wayne had contracted any disease we weren't aware of, my parents would be spared additional grief.

There's no way of knowing the detailed findings of when they went to harvest Wayne's organs. However, when they called the following week to tell my parents how the procedure went, they were told that nothing was salvageable due to an infection.

Since I didn't know Wayne well, I didn't analyze the situation with the calling card. Wayne was known to have had a sarcastic sense of humor around people he was comfortable hanging with, and he enjoyed cracking jokes. It's possible that the calling card was just a joke. To my knowledge, I was the only one who knew about the card unless Mom found more and decided this was a "don't say anything to Dad" scenario. It would have been her style to keep it a secret from everyone.

I don't believe it was coincidental that I was sitting next to my Dad when the white calling card dropped on the dark carpeted floor. I don't think it was happenstance that my Mom was sitting across from us in the funeral home lobby area, yet she didn't notice something dropped on the floor. I don't believe it was luck that I stopped short of leaving the hospital that day without asking for information to be kept from my folks that could have been damaging and grievous for them to learn of their son. God is mindful of us and cares about even the most minor details of our lives.

That's What Love Looks Like. #CARING!

CHAPTER 17

Let the Walls Come Tumbling Down

I'm thinking back to when in my early twenties, my Dad had been falsely accused of causing dissension in a Christian organization. I remember being in the meeting where these erroneous charges were brought before the men, and it was decided to disfellowship my Dad from the group. Before the decision, several of us, including myself, had expressed that what they were doing was wrong. I tearfully begged them to not proceed. It was tough to witness and then to see those at fault continue with "business as usual" as if nothing had happened.

Years passed, and I had forgiven those involved in the deceitful action. I had even gone to the leader of the organization years later, and close to the end of his life, I had told him I loved him and didn't hold anything against him for what had happened. Amends had been made, so I thought.

I had left that specific location within the organization to return to it a few years later. While worshiping the Lord one night in that building where the meeting against my Dad had taken place, God showed me how I had built a wall of protection so that others couldn't get too close and I'd be spared of future hurts. The structure I had built over the years had almost completed, with just the roof left to be put on. God told me if I didn't give the hurt to Him, I wouldn't be able to hear Him speak clearly into my life.

I fell to my knees, and I wept before Him. I gave Him all the hurt and the need to keep others at a distance. That night, He healed me. Though there have been times since I can feel myself trying to pull away from others, I'm aware that to love like He loves, you can't do it at a distance, and relationships can be messy. Life in general is messy, isn't it?!?

To love anyone involves vulnerability because that someone may disappoint, walk away, or pass away. And if you allow yourself to love, British author and theologian C.S. Lewis, in The Four Loves, said, your heart will likely be "wrung and possibly broken." Suppose you want to make sure that never happens. In that case, he says you'll have to "lock it up safe in the casket or coffin of your selfishness" where it's "safe, dark, motionless, airless…" In that place, it will become "unbreakable, impenetrable, irredeemable." Wow!

Think of how putting yourself in that place of lockdown and all the opportunities of strengthening current friendships and making new friends are lost. Sharing our lives with others is how love is expressed. People aren't blessed when we hide away in a protective shell. I'm glad God spoke to me that day, or I would have finished off the roof and been all alone. He could have left me alone, but He didn't, and so many great things that have happened in my life since then, including writing this book, wouldn't have come about.

That's What Love Looks Like. #FORESIGHT!

CHAPTER 18

Father Really Does Know Best

Looking back more than eight years, I see how God directed my life so perfectly. If I had bought a house as I wanted, I would have had to work full-time to cover my daily living expenses. That is huge because from 2011 to mid-2019, I needed to be available for my Mom and Dad and wouldn't have been able to do for them while being employed full time. In this time frame, I was able to get their finances in order, help Mom transition to taking over the household responsibilities that Dad always managed, and move them closer to my new location. I was able to be with Mom as Dad's health continued to decline, which led to placing Dad in a nursing home. I was with them several days a week until my Dad passed away, which wouldn't have been possible if I had bought a house or the duplex. On top of all this, since October 2016, life has become even more interesting, with my brother getting a diagnosis that rocked my world!

I tell you this and the rest of the stories in this book to share *what love looks like.* God IS love. Yesterday, I was getting some exercise, walking along the bay and taking in the beauty of the diamonds dancing on the water as the sun shone brightly on its surface. The sight was breathtaking, and I realized how fortunate I am and have been in reaping the rewards of being one of God's children.

As I was enjoying the dancing diamonds, I reflected on the past six months and how I became semi-retired in my early 50s with the time-freedoms that come with retirement. I didn't volunteer for early retirement or starting over as a second-time divorcee. But God was orchestrating things for His perfect purposes in my life, from the layoff to the move to renting a house.

In the great times and in the not-so-good times, God is really showing me *What Love Looks Like. #DESTINY!*

Divine Connections

Unexpected Encounters, Angels in Disguise, & Faith Restored

CHAPTER 19

Falling Into my Father's Arms

Dad has gotten combative, so it is time to put him into a facility where he can get the proper care and my Mom's safety isn't compromised. At this point, I hadn't moved my folks; they were six and a half hours drive from me. As my Mom was admitting him to his new "home," I was driving to her place to support her. It would be THE most difficult thing she ever had to do, but I wasn't expecting it to be as horrific as it was.

I'll never forget walking into my folks' house and my Mom collapsing into my arms. We held each other for minutes and sobbed. She was hurting so badly for Dad, and my heart felt like it would explode with the grief of seeing her hurt.

I went to my bedroom, crying uncontrollably. I cried out to God in anguish. I needed Him, at that moment, to take the grief from me; I felt like I would die. Shortly after that, I experienced something that comes only from above. It was like a blanket wrapped around me as I fell into my heavenly Father's arms.

That's What Love Looks Like. #COMFORT!

CHAPTER 20

The Food Pantry

About a year after coming to the Florida panhandle, I felt the release to return to the workforce and a mutual contact that my pastor friend had, wanted to start a food pantry. I agreed to take on this endeavor, even though I had no idea what it would entail. I never visited a food pantry, didn't rub shoulders with anyone who needed a food pantry, and was clueless about what a successfully run food pantry looked like.

After visiting three food pantries to see how things are done elsewhere, we opened up the pantry with 35 volunteers, and within three weeks, we were serving over 350 families. Our clientele was getting their food needs met and we even had a prayer room available for anyone who wanted prayer while waiting in line to pick up their food. New friends were made and we saw many touched by God's presence and provision.

I started working the job in April 2012 when, eight to nine months later, the Lord told me I needed to resign. He and I had a very brief conversation that went something like this:

Me: "God, I'm just learning what love looks like. Why would you have me quit this job when I have so much more to learn?"

God: "Because I want you to write your book, and I want to birth new songs in you."

Me: "Okay."

I immediately wrote my resignation and emailed it to my boss before I would change my mind. This obedience thing was becoming a great habit! Was I beginning to get the hang of this trust-and-obey thing?

I went to bed, and as soon as I hit the mattress, the lyrics to a new song and the tune downloaded to me. I love it when God confirms things so quickly! So the song wouldn't be forgotten, I grabbed a device to record it.

It took a couple of months for the replacement staff to get hired and trained, and the last week was difficult for me. Even though everything good that came out of the food pantry was because I sought God in how to do things, I had formed an identity tied to what I was doing there. One afternoon, I remember speaking to the Lord, "I hope I'm on track. I hope I'm on track."

A few hours after praying that prayer, I went to a church service where an out-of-town minister named Tim was the guest speaker. We had never met, and he didn't know any details about me, but God knew I needed assurance about leaving the food pantry job. Just before Tim delivered his message, he spoke directly to me after calling me out of the crowd and said these exact words: that "God wants you to know you're RIGHT ON TRACK." Then he said three times, "Stay the course." Wow! God is so good.

That's What Love Looks Like. #DOUBLE*CONFIRMATION!

CHAPTER 21

In the Middle

Have you ever wanted something even though you knew it wasn't the best for you and would have a negative outcome? This has been my case a few times, and then God changed my heart. I mean, a 180-degree change when I couldn't help myself. And just a side note here – the saying "God only helps those who help themselves" is incorrect! I often couldn't help myself, and that's when crying out to God while admitting my inadequacy opened me up to receive His help.

One of the times I was in that predicament was around 2015. I had been seeing a guy who didn't respect some boundaries I had communicated and had told him if we were to continue seeing one another, things had to change on his part. After the second incident, I didn't need to continue to see him; however, my flesh wanted to be gratified. A war raged inside me that desired to be treasured, honored, and valued, but not at the expense of compromising Biblical values.

I remember needing to end the relationship and, at the same time, wanting to continue to see him. I went to church on a Wednesday night, knowing my heart wasn't in the right place. I went into the church and started praying while the others were in the fellowship hall having a Bible study. I shared my feelings with the Lord, telling Him I wanted to want Him more than I wanted "the guy" while simultaneously wanting the opposite. After asking God to change my heart, I then joined the others when the pastor was teaching about setting our affections on things above and not on things that are on the earth and temporal.[16]

After the Bible study, I asked the church to pray for me. I had to do something difficult the next day, and I needed God to continue working in my heart so I wouldn't accept the second best in my life.

The next day, "the guy" picked me up to go to the mall with him, and I immediately realized just as God removed the desire from me for the duplex, I had NO desire to be with him. I helped him pick out some clothes for an important event he was attending in a couple of days, but it was undeniable that God had done what I asked Him to do. It never ceases to amaze me how God can change a heart when the heart is handed over to Him. He not only changed my desires, but I realized I am already treasured, already valued, and already honored by the One that matters the most. That's more than good enough for me. *That's What Real Love Looks Like!*

The inspiration for the following poem came from a sermon I heard on YouTube of Jesus' disciples who faced a big storm in a boat on their way to meet Jesus.[17] Jesus had already told them that He would meet them on the other side of the lake. Though that should have been enough reason to know that the storm wouldn't be fatal, they were afraid when they were in the thick of the giant waves. In the middle of the storm, Jesus shows up for the disciples.

God often gives us instructions and promises of a great outcome, but when we're in the middle of going from Point A to Point B, we can get fearful. Sometimes, we may feel alone or have bouts of doubt. We may even work hard to combat the waves and storms surrounding us. We can experience Jesus in the middle like in no other place in our daily walk with him. It's in the middle that we mature and get stronger in Him, experiencing the power of His presence. I was "in the middle" when I wrote this poem on 8/14/2015 to encourage myself shortly after ending the above mentioned relationship.

"In the Middle but Still Yours" By DiLeigh Grace:

A voice tells me to call on the fellow.
This happens when I'm feeling not so mellow.

I've been in a pit. It seems like forever.
Depression, regression, the enemy's been pretty clever.

But in the middle of all this, I hear my Father's voice.
His voice is different than the others:
"Call on ME", He says, "I'm the right choice".

I'm always waiting on you to show you you're special.
Treasured, honored, and valued like fine metals.

I'm preparing you, touching your heart.
But do not fear, for there are some broken parts.

At times, it can be painful, and it seems like a slow process.
But know I'm working in your life, and together, we're making progress.

As I lovingly pry and the tears you cry,
the work I'm doing is amazing for I'm brewing.

I'm mixing in My love with sprinkles of joy
in just the right amounts, enough that you can enjoy.

Then I add peace, how sweet and serene.
You'd think you were sleeping and having a sweet dream.

All of these things I created for you,
so you can experience heaven on earth and share me with others, too.

Working out the kinks on a continual basis,
it takes time to take you through the desert to my secret oasis.

And when our time in the current desert is through,
after many drinks of Me, you'll feel brand new.

No feeling used or worn, shattered or torn,
only a work of my Spirit.

Hold on with all you have,
not to worldly ideals, but hold on to me.

Trust Me, let Me love you,
then it's Me leading you, you will see.

There's coming a day when you'll feel full strength restored.
Continue to stay connected through My love, your umbilical cord.

You've always been mine, even before you were formed.
I will never, ever abandon you, especially in future storms.

It's part of your story, so don't forget where you've been.
Don't try to put on the spin.

Keep your eyes open and your heart, too.
For I will reach out to others, reaching out through you.

In the middle, *That's What Love Looks Like. #TRUSTING!*

CHAPTER 22

Divorced and Displaced

In 2012, I was divorced from my husband #2 of over 12 years. I was devastated and didn't want to fall into another trap of looking for love (or lust) in all the wrong places, as I did after my first divorce. I needed to keep my eyes on the Lord, and so that's what my intention was.

It was now August 15, 2015, and I was at the beach walking. And I couldn't stop uncontrollably weeping as I witnessed families together, playing with one another and enjoying each other's company. I wanted that so much for myself and was reeling with emotions. I went home and wrote this poem:

"Broken" By DiLeigh Grace:

In our vows, we said, "I do."
Through thick and thin, we would become kin.

The growing sexual desires were out of control.
I thought it was normal, yet it was damaging the soul.

Never was there enough of me to give to him.
No matter what I did, it didn't quench the beast of sin.

On the outside, we looked good. I honored and loved him.
We had the world by the tail, and yet things grew more grim.

More was required of me, and the physical needs were spoken.
But all I gave was received like small tokens.

The first seven years were pretty rough for me,
I was carrying a ball and chain, things I didn't see.

The ball was shame, and the chain was pride,
baggage of a prior divorce, and to Jesus, I cried.

I went to a ladies retreat where I found sweet relief,
so glad Jesus saw my pain and set me free from shame.

I came home like a bird set free!
But I could see the enemy wasn't happy,
I could see it in his eyes when he looked at me.

Two months later, cancer came, and treatments started.
I felt lots of sorrow, and I felt fainthearted.

I could barely keep on my feet.
During the four months of treatment, I napped a lot
and listened to Christian music frequently.

My faith in God grew as I worshiped him in new freedom.
But then the verbal abuse started. There was no rhyme, no reason.

After four more years, I left, not knowing the end result.
Leaving a note, reaching out and without insults.

For more than a year, I was hoping he would understand.
But pornography had a tight grip. The addiction is like quicksand.

The insults continued, no reconciliation to be found.
He filed for a divorce. No longer would he be bound,

It's as if I didn't exist, those twelve years we were together.
He just threw them and me away like a piece of shoe leather.

Sometimes, the grief is so real, and the emotions are raw.
There's been no remorse, no regrets I saw.

It's been almost three years since the divorce.
And tonight, on the beach, the tears were not forced.

The tears kept coming as if a dam had broke.
I wanted it to be so different, but to him, we were just a bad joke.

You'd think I'd be over the losses by now.
But when I see families together, it rips my heart like a plow.

Tonight, I prayed to God, "I am hurting so!
I give you my life; it's all to You I owe!"

"I give You permission, Lord, to mend my heart.
Every broken piece I give You, yes, every single part".

"As you continue to mold me and make things anew,
let me always be mindful that You are Faithful, You are True".

Yesterday was the first day I had broken into a smile.
I'd forgotten what it was like, for it had been quite a while.

Lately, I've been praying for my joy to be restored.
I know my strength and real joy comes from the Lord.

I'm looking for better days ahead,
as I sing His praises that go through my head.

God's been taking what the enemy meant for evil,
His love pouring in and out of me is lethal.

I may have cried a bucket of tears today,
but because of Him, this brokenness cannot stay.

Come quickly, Lord Jesus. Come and take us home.
But until that great day, don't let my devotion to you roam.

You paid the ultimate price so I could be free.
But it's going to cost me everything. You want everything, all of me.

Broken, I am Yours!

That's What Love Looks Like. #DESPERATION!

CHAPTER 23

Useful Not Useless

Below is an excerpt from a Facebook post I made on 8/16/2015:

I just read something that could change your life drastically or that of someone you know. Perhaps you look at someone divorced and think they're damaged or less than. If you or someone you know has been through a divorce, know that God can and desires to use them, yes, even after such a loss. How do I know this with ALL certainty?

There's a famous story you might have heard several times, but perhaps you missed an essential piece of its meaning, as I have. It's about a woman who had been married five times and lived with a man when she met Jesus at a well where she was drawing water in the heat of the day to avoid the others who shunned her due to her reputation. Jesus told her that He was the long-awaited Messiah. After her eyes of understanding were opened, she ran into town. She told everyone about Him, encouraging them to come and see for themselves this man who knew everything about her. Because of this five-time divorcee's testimony, Jesus stayed with them for two more days, and many people in her town became believers. All because of the life-changing words Jesus spoke that started with this woman.[18]

There were others that discovered Jesus was the Promised One. There were shepherds and wise men that came to worship the Christ child.[19] Also, it was two elderly people named Anna and Simeon who were in the temple that had been waiting a long time with expectancy for their coming Messiah.[20] God revealed Jesus' identity to them. But it was a divorced woman of five husbands and full of shame that was one of the first to get a revelation of who this Jesus was and then ran to tell others.

Did Jesus not take a bad situation in this woman's life and turn it around for His (and her) good? Why didn't Jesus go further into town and find someone with a better reputation to spread the news of His love?

God looks into the heart. He didn't see her for what she had done in the past but for who He created her to be! And this same news is true today. It doesn't matter what we've done in the past. He loves us and sees what we can become when we place our lives in His hands with complete trust! When He can take a woman living in much shame, open her eyes to see her need for a Savior and redeem her, then turn her into one of the first missionaries, God can use you, and God can use me.

That's What Love Looks Like. #MERCY!

CHAPTER 24

Life Isn't for the Weak

Love doesn't quit. When it's challenging, when it's tough, it's love that pulls us through situations. It's what can control our response to a God who gave us His all so that we can have a vibrant relationship with Him through His son, Jesus. I wrote the following poem on New Year's Day, 2016.

"Finishing Strong" By DiLeigh Grace:

Another year has come and gone.
I'm not so sure I still have my song.

I feel slightly bummed that there should have been more.
Was last year to be tagged as a dud, a big bore?

I just finished listening to Tony Evans on Finishing Strong.
I want to live life in 2016 right and less wrong.

With every New Year comes a recollection of the last.
It's not to own me, but I feel compelled to look at the past.

2015 has had its ups and downs.
But God has never failed, He's always been around.

I can think of lives I have touched for His good.
People He's put in front of me, just because He could.

There were a few times I expected more to show up at my house.
Only one or two would come, but they're more valuable than a mouse.

God would orchestrate the whole thing.
Sometimes I would sit at the piano and sing.

We would talk about essential oils, but I know the real goal
is to be a blessing for my Father and for them to fulfill His role.

We all have a mission in this life, and it's to thrive
Oh God, how I want to be more than just alive!

The past year has been a difficult one.
The book's still not written. It's not nearly done.

My prayer since January 2013 has been, "I hope I'm on track."
I don't understand what God's doing, but I know He's got my back.

"To stay the course" is the edict God gave me
and I'm more determined to become what I'm meant to be.

I still feel pretty stuck in the middle with a pinch of strife,
but I think it's a transition from the desert to real life.

Life with purpose, life with joy, life with a burning passion.
To accomplish God's best is a thought that may sound old-fashioned.

But it doesn't matter what others may think.
I just don't want my life to stink.

With the same old, same old, dullness and numbness,
the God I serve definitely has no dumbness.

I've seen Him work in my life dozens of times.
And there's no way I will abandon Him, shine in me God, shine!

After listening to Tony's sermon, I prayed,
"What lights my fire? Speak to me, Your handmaid."

"What is it that makes me smile from the inside out?"
and He quietly answered me, not with a shout.

I'm going to be obedient in what He has spoken.
"Use me, O God, I don't like being broken".

I know I have made some progress this past year.
Not all was a waste. I surely will not fear.

I give You my discouragement, my goals, and my dreams.
My life belongs to You, no more of the enemy's schemes.

If it takes me hours and hours each day,
in Your presence is where I will wait, is where I will stay.

I cried for weeks as I thought I'd missed out.
And indeed I had, there is no doubt.

I lost out on lust which is very selfish, very self-centered.
I am so much more, I am valued, and I'm treasured.

My heart was hurt as I nearly gave it to another.
But God, You rescued me from chains that only kill, only smother.

I learned much from this last relationship;
no one should have that much of a grip.

24/7 my thoughts were consumed with him.
He became an idol, and the future looked very grim.

I'm glad I walked away from a counterfeit love.
I choose the God of true love when push comes to shove.

I just got off the phone with a new friend Irene.
She's a super lady, and her mind is so keen.

She reminded me of the many friends I had made this past year.
I really am blessed, and I will count each one as dear.

So thank you, Lord, for these gifts. These friends so true.
I'm surrounded by some great people, not just one or two.

So, as I look back, I truly can say,
It's not been a bad year, and I'm still the clay.

Clay needs a potter who knows what He's doing.
I'm His daughter, and it is He I am pursuing.

I will trust and not be afraid.
With His life's blood, my sin's penalty He paid.

I will run this race, steady though slow.
FINISHING STRONG, staying low.

Looking back, I can see a heart surrendering to
a God constantly reaching out to me.

That's What Love Looks Like. #DETERMINATION!

CHAPTER 25

Broken No More

I'm thinking about the word Broken. One definition is weakened and feeble. I think of a piece of pottery that's smashed and broken into many parts.

The wisest man in the world, King Solomon, once said that sorrow of the heart causes a broken spirit[21] and a broken spirit hurts to the bone[22] BUT God is near those with a broken heart and saves those crushed in spirit![23]

A little over five months after I wrote the poem Broken, I penned the following poem.

"Broken No More" By DiLeigh Grace:

Today, 1/31/16, it dawned on me that the pain is gone.
I don't know when it happened. I just know I have moved on.

I gave Him permission to mend my heart,
and the broken pieces were healed, the big and small parts.

How do I know a healing has taken place?
Sadness is gone, and I'm experiencing His grace.

Daily, I see His hand in my life.
Joy is growing, and grief doesn't cut like a knife.

The world all around is swirling in confusion,
but I know it's due to Satan's lies and illusions.

It's in the Word that the truth is revealed.
And God's faith working in us is our shield.

There's no room for doubt or fear of tomorrow,
as I keep my eyes on Him, His plans He will show.

One day, very soon, the kingdoms of this world will fall
and all the temporal things we hold dear will seem so small.

We can hardly imagine the new heavens and earth,
it's just one of many rewards of the second birth.

It's not the swift that runs well in this race,
but it's the one that keeps getting up when they fall on their face.

Broken, I may have been; it's part of my past.
But I'm broken no more, and I'm free at last.

There is so much more in my life for Him to do,
and it's on my knees where He will see me through.

I will let Him work on me on the potter's wheel.
Even there, He shows me His love is so very real.

Thank you, God, for the joy you've restored.
Use my life so others will know You as Lord!

A life that's been transformed is *What Love Looks Like.*
#HEALING!

CHAPTER 26

Stay or Move? That is the Question!

Two days ago, 11/13/17, I planned on moving across town to a newly built apartment complex. The deal seemed great. I could save $300 - $450 a month, get an extra bedroom and bathroom, and have lots of closet space with the dreams of getting rid of my portable closet in the tiny house I currently live in. I would have 49 other families close by in the apartment complex, and I thought of how I might be able to bring value to these families.

I put my application in, and then I waited. Getting approval for the move and the apartment unit assigned to me was rough. It would typically take a week to get approved, and it was more than three weeks before I received the first phone call saying everything was all set. Then I was told twice that the specific apartment being held for me was NOT the one for me, and then the phone call came that announced I was approved, but the apartment was on the second floor.

I am faced with a dilemma because the apartment office is requiring an answer within 24 hours. Being on the second floor and having 15 concrete steps between floors is problematic since I often lugged stuff back and forth to my car and Mom's place. I have continued to seek God and increase the time I spend with Him, for I cannot handle the stresses involving my brother and my Dad in my own strength. I have a longing for Him with the realization that I cannot live without Him. He's like the very air I need to breathe. I will get back to my brother in a moment. I needed God's will for me to be revealed regarding this move.

I was getting ready to go to a women's Bible study and had about 45 minutes, so I sat in my living room, still before Him. I told Him I was here and listening to Him, and then I just sat. It seemed the heavens were shut, and I didn't get any response, so I went to the front yard. I paced back and forth, waiting to hear some advice on this matter of moving. I confessed to Him I only wanted His best while thinking His best was for me to move. I couldn't see any downsides to moving other than the stairs. However, God knew something (well, lots of things) I didn't know. I knew God had led me to the dog choir neighborhood and knew that His timing was perfect. I truly wanted what He wanted more than I liked the apartment, and I liked the apartment pretty, pretty bad.

In my pacing, I asked God to speak to me clearly so I'd know what to do. I reminded Him of the deadline (like He didn't already know). It was time for me to leave for the Bible study, and I was trying to think through how I would hear God's answer when it came to me. And I thought of Gideon in the Bible and how he put out a fleece before God. So I told God if I heard someone speak specifically to me with one of two words, I would know what to do.

I was trying to listen intently as I hung on to every word that was spoken to me. I'm sure I looked like I was in pain. Have you ever noticed that look of intensity that sometimes people have when they are deep in thought? That was me that night. During the Beth Moore Bible study video on how Life is Complicated, I heard her lean on the podium and say one of the words I asked God to use to communicate to me.

Doubt came quickly behind this, and I asked God for another confirmation. Oh, how patient God must be with me at times like these! And with you too, I am guessing. I told Him, "Maybe I missed it, God. Maybe you said the other word earlier, and that's what You want me to do." On my drive home from the Bible study, I decided to see if the teaching was available on YouTube to listen to it again.

The words I had asked God to use in giving me the answer were LEAVE and STAY. The word I thought I heard Beth say was STAY. When I got home, I found the teaching and pressed play. I never did find the original place where I thought I heard her say, "STAY with me now." However, I found in two statements back to back where she spoke the word STAY three times and then once more in the following statement.

I had gotten my answer even though it wasn't the one I wanted to hear. But that was okay. I didn't want to sleep on it or change my mind, so even though it was after hours and I'd get the answering machine, I quickly called the apartment office and left a voicemail message stating I would need to pass on the apartment. I also notified my landlord and told them I was not moving and would stay in their rental house.

The following day, I let my Mom and a dear friend know that I had turned down the apartment, and they both told me I might not want to unpack my boxes. I was to soon find out why, but it was interesting that when I questioned them later why they told me not to unpack, my Mom didn't recall telling me that, and my friend didn't know why he advised me that way. If God can use a donkey to talk to a prophet, I reckon He can use two of my closest friends to talk to me!

God is patient and wants those of us seeking Him for answers to receive what we need. I continue to practice contentment as I remind myself that having Him is most important.

Loving the Lord our God with all of our heart is identifying what is in the heart and then deciding that you want God more. It's in the heart where desires hang out. Our desires determine how we spend our time, and what we think about directly impacts our actions.

That's What True Love Looks Like. #GUIDANCE!

CHAPTER 27

Butterflies and Boxes

So here I was in the rental house with things partially packed and wondering why I shouldn't unpack. I started unpacking some of the books, placing them back onto the bookcase shelves, when I was impressed to stop. A few days later, I got a phone call from the apartments, and they said they had a first-floor apartment available for me if I wanted to take it.

I told the apartment manager I would be right over to look at it, and as I made the short drive to the property, I prayed again for God to show me what to do. It was in October, and I hadn't seen a butterfly for months. I decided if I saw a butterfly, I would take that as a sign I was to take flight and make the move. As I drove into the property, I saw something fly in front of my car, but it was a dragonfly. So far, it was a no.

I got the key from the manager, walked into the apartment, and noticed it was a handicap unit. That was strange because the original apartment they had for me was handicapped. Since my application didn't specify I needed a handicap unit and they told me I couldn't change the application, they couldn't rent it to me. Instead of returning to the office and questioning this finding, I walked to the back of the apartments to worship. I was alert and watching to see what His answer was for me. Out of nowhere, this butterfly came at me, dove into the ground, and vanished. First off, this is the first time I have seen a butterfly dive into the ground before or since then. And never has one disappeared into thin air as fast as it came. I continued to worship because I desired the move but was not convinced it was the best decision. Then I saw it; I mean them. THREE butterflies together, and all three of them were different. I was so excited because I felt God's favor and blessing on the decision to move. And the number three biblically represents divine wholeness, completeness, and perfection. The number three was used to put a divine stamp of approval on my move.

I then went to the apartment office and asked the manager if she knew that the unit was handicapped. She said yes, and after I reminded her of the prior conversation about me not getting a handicapped unit, she reassured me it was mine if I wanted it. So, the deal was signed, sealed, and delivered to me! Now I knew why I wasn't supposed to unpack, but getting myself moved would take significant doing since I had only ten days to do it. I also had to call my current landlord to tell them I was moving. After calling them twice before telling them I was moving and then not moving, I wasn't sure they would believe me!

One of the reasons I wanted to move to the new apartments had to do with my budget. I needed to lower my living expenses, and the only area I could see I could do that was reduce my housing expenses. And though I was comfortable where I was and made some new friends, I felt that my time was up in living there. My God is a good, good Father, and I am so loved by Him as He shows me a way of provision that wasn't feasible in a town with a shortage of rental properties.

That's What Love Looks Like. #CLARITY!

Embracing Unconditional Love

A Journey of Spiritual Discovery, Unveiling God's Love, & Embracing Self-Love

CHAPTER 28

You are My Dad and I am Your Daughter

I am finishing this chapter on 11/4/17 and want to insert a poem I wrote in the early morning hours on 9/25/16. This was less than six months before my Dad's death on May 1, 2017. I had been up all morning struggling with negative memories of my Dad and questioning why God kept him on this earth when Alzheimer's had ravaged his mind. I was extremely frustrated and didn't see any purpose in his remaining here. This particular morning, when I asked God why He hadn't taken my Dad to his eternal home, I was surprised when it was made clear to me that I was one of the reasons. I needed to eliminate the bad memories of conflict with my Dad.

Then, my mind was flooded with all the great things about my Dad and how he enriched my life. My Dad and I had an amazing relationship. I was his only daughter and I loved him dearly. There wasn't a thing we wouldn't do for one another; however, we were both hard-headed at times and this would cause some unnecessary friction. Though the ugly moments were just a few, my greatest concern was that I would only have the bad memories remain after he would pass. I needed to see all the wonderful things about him and as the words of this poem just flowed out of me, the bad thoughts were swallowed up by all the good. I was reminded that many of his great qualities were so much a part of who I had become.

"You are my Dad and I am Your Daughter!" By DiLeigh Grace:

Today, I have learned a little more about grace,
about God's love reflected in this time and this place.
For on this earth there are mistakes we make,
but to overlook them is a choice we can take.

I started to reflect on the many good things that make you, you.
And Dad there may not be enough time to list them, they are not a few.

The times that you worked many long hours;
we never did without food, clothing, or electrical power.
This is the Dad I choose to remember,
cause you are my Dad and I am your daughter!

And when I was 15 and you rededicated your life to the Lord,
here I am many years later, recalling the many
smiles on your face I cannot ignore.
This is the Dad I choose to remember,
cause you are my Dad and I am your daughter!

When your parents were ill and needed a helping hand,
it wasn't something that you saw coming,
it wasn't something you planned.

You made many sacrifices and I never saw any displeasure.
I didn't know until decades later it cost
everything, all of your monetary treasures.
This is the Dad I choose to remember,
cause you are my Dad and I am your daughter!

You have taught me many lessons, some I've learned really well.
Like how to stretch a dollar and how to dig for clam shells.
I remember the times when you were at the helm of the boat.
How I loved to sit at the bow and watch the seaweed float.
This is the Dad I choose to remember,
cause you are my Dad and I am your daughter!

You're one of the very few people who can purchase something used,
then turn around and sell it for more as if it's new and improved.
This is the Dad I choose to remember,
cause you are my Dad and I am your daughter!

Some of the things I have mentioned here,
appear to be all about things in the earthly sphere.
And even though you were a former
banker and businessman, Dad,
you lived a life of principle and integrity more valuable than fads.
This is the Dad I choose to remember,
cause you are my Dad and I am your daughter!

Four years ago we had a conversation.
It was about your mind wanting to go on a vacation.
I told you there may come a day when you wouldn't know my name,
but you reminded me you'd never forget me inside
your heart, things would never change.
This is the Dad I choose to remember,
cause you are my Dad and I am your daughter!

Time on this earth goes very, very fast
so let's build a few more memories that will forever last.
I look forward to seeing things like the pearl of great price,
for He's in each of us, the pearl is Jesus Christ.
This is the Dad I choose to remember,
cause you are my Dad and I am your daughter!

I have a feeling that soon you will trade
the old body for the new, no longer decayed.
There will be no memory loss and no more sorrows to endure,
and in His presence, there will be only joy, that's for sure.
This is the Dad I choose to remember,
cause you are my Dad and I am your daughter!

The past four years have not been without struggles
but I value you more now than if life had been without troubles.
I realized today I have been richly blessed
with every new day that you can hold me to your chest.
This is the Dad I choose to remember,
cause God is my Father and I am His daughter!

If you were to look at a photo of my Dad and me, you would see how much I look like my Dad. Based on physical resemblances, there would be no question that I am his daughter. People meeting me for the first time would notice this likeness when they saw us together.

Just as my earthly Dad taught me many things, he and my heavenly Father began teaching me things very early, and these lessons continue today. The more I learn, the more I realize I don't know. Some days, it seems as if I have never opened God's letters to me (His Word aka the Bible). He continues teaching me things as if I've never read any of the familiar words previously. And in many cases, I've read them multiple times.

Is there a resemblance between me and my heavenly Father today? Is what I have learned and continue to learn changing me from the inside out so that not only do I "look" like Him, but my actions and words coming out of my mouth cause people to say, "She's just like her heavenly Father?!?" May this be our reality for those who claim to be Christ-followers. This is my desire, and I hope my experiences and the life lessons I share within these pages will bless you and make an eternal impact.

I was encouraged to think of all the positive, beautiful things about my Dad. Before my Dad left this earth for his heavenly home, I shared this poem with him and told him how much I loved him.

That's What Love Looks Like! #REVEALING!

CHAPTER 29

Help! I've Fallen and I Can't Get Up!

Dad was in nursing home #1 for a few months when he attempted to escape by using a chair to get him over a fence on the backside of the property. This was the best thing that happened to us! He had a minor injury, which landed him in the ER. And thanks to the ER doctor who saw he needed a medication change, his aggressive behavior decreased enough that we could bring him home. It's now 2016, and we've cared for Dad at home for several years. When we took him out of nursing home #1, I asked Mom to seriously consider readmitting Dad if and when caring for him started taking a toll on her health. We put him on a wait list at one of the nation's best VA nursing homes with a memory care unit. Though this facility gave excellent care, it was still a hard decision. We had turned down admitting him many other times, but during Christmas week, we got the call that a bed had become available, and it was time.

My Mom said moving her and Dad to the Florida panhandle was the best move they ever made, and one of the reasons was the excellent care he was receiving. Not only had I moved to a place I continue to call my paradise, but my folks also benefited from the relocation. God truly took the lousy situation of going through a divorce and turning things to my family's advantage. He never ceases to amaze me!

Dad's receiving excellent care, and we visit him several times weekly. It's 2017, and Mom, who is 88 years old, has fallen. She's broken her back so she is taken to the hospital via ambulance. She opted out of surgery and decided to give her back a chance to heal on its own while she wore a brace that made her look like a turtle. I go to call my two brothers to let them know what's going on when I find out that my brother Bruce is being taken from work to the hospital emergency room, 6.5 hours from us.

I'm going back and forth between the hospital to see Mom and check in with Dad at the nursing home, which is just 20 minutes between the two of them. The hospital wants to discharge Mom, but she can't be left alone. She was in no condition to join me in driving to see about my brother. It was Thursday around 4 p.m. when I requested that the hospital find my Mom an inpatient rehab facility bed so I could get to my brother the following morning. I'm told it will be impossible to find her a bed that quickly, especially since it is coming to the close of the business day. I asked them to try because we had prayed, and I was confident that something would open up for us.

The hospital employee returns within 20 minutes, and he's scratching his head, telling me he can't believe he found a place to take my Mom that night! He processed her discharge papers and transferred her to the rehab facility in a few hours.

I trusted our God to come through for us and He showed us AGAIN that this is *What Love Looks Like. #TIMELY!*

CHAPTER 30

Not Again!! You Have to be Kidding Me!

Bruce's trip to the hospital was due to him not remembering what to do at his job, which was repetitive work that he could do just fine for several years.

Bruce had been in two severe car accidents about 15 years earlier. In those accidents, he suffered concussions and sustained neck and back injuries. After those accidents, his behavior changed, but we just thought it was Bruce's response to life's bumps in the road.

A few weeks before his work-related hospital visit, we noticed things weren't right with his reasoning, ability to follow instructions, and short-term memory. He was also asking us the same questions repeatedly during conversations with us. And his neighbors had shared some odd behaviors they had witnessed along with increased signs of memory loss.

Bruce is five years older than me and at this time he's only 62 years old. With the death of my oldest brother and because of the history of dementia and brain aneurysms on both sides of my parents' families, Mom and I were deeply concerned. It was only months before Dad passed away when the neurologist diagnosed Bruce as having early stages of Alzheimer's. I couldn't believe we would go through another bout with this disease. I hated it with a vengeance and couldn't believe this was happening! Again!

We wanted a second opinion. By this time, Mom could travel, so she and I took Bruce to another neurologist and had some diagnostic tests done to eliminate other possible causes for his symptoms. He also went through six hours of verbal communication testing with a psychological neurologist. Each time, the diagnosis was confirmed, and my heart was aching.

Bruce lived alone, which meant some hard decisions had to be made. I thought we had more time to figure things out because the disease can take years to worsen to the point of the patient needing additional assistance, but that wasn't the case. Not this time.

Bruce was a smoker who owned motorcycles, drove a car, and lived in a mobile home that could go up in flames in seconds if he smoked a cigarette in his house and forgot about it. Though I was quite a distance drive from him, the only other sibling of ours lived further away, so I was the one who needed to see that he was cared for.

Shortly after Bruce's diagnosis, we got a call from one of his neighbors that Bruce had been in an accident. He had wrecked his motorcycle and didn't know where the cycle was. He didn't remember what happened. He was very confused. He had already taken two doses of medication by accident at the recent visit to our Mom's place, so his living alone wouldn't work. Until I could arrange things for him to move, his neighbor would keep close tabs on him and administer his meds.

Before we made any final commitments to admit Bruce to a facility, we found the one we thought would suit him best and then had Bruce come and look at it. Not only was it just five minutes drive from my Mom's place, but the style and layout of the facility resembled his prior living conditions. He was excited that he wouldn't have to cook any of his meals or do his laundry, and he liked the place. He was thrilled that he'd have one of the largest private rooms and have enough space for his stereo equipment. This was important to him and we were delighted that he had such a positive outlook with this upcoming change!

There was much that had to be done before moving Bruce. Getting insurance benefits lined up for an assisted living facility involved managing his finances. I also had to go through all my brother's belongings, decide what was non-essential so those items could be sold in a yard sale or consigned so we'd have the funds to keep utilities on until his property sold.

While we were staging the house to be put on the market in the central Florida summer heat, we had water pipes bust twice, and the A/C compressor broke down two times. During the second of three or four trips to Bruce's place, we had to leave immediately after receiving a call that Dad had had a stroke and was taken to the hospital. We headed back home, and Dad never recovered. We stayed by his side until the Lord received him to Himself.

Bruce was moved to a facility, and everything, including the mobile home sale, was done in about 12 months. I was so thankful I could be there for my folks and brother. I could again see how God had directed my steps as He promised when we trust Him and acknowledge Him in everything we do.[24] He also reminded me that not only had he hand-picked me to be my Dad's daughter, but he specifically selected me to be my brother's sister, too.

This is What Love Looks Like in being a daughter of the One that knows the future. *#CHOSEN!*

CHAPTER 31

He Loves Me, He Loves Me NOT!

Before I moved Bruce to the facility where he could get needed care, I started researching CTE (Chronic Traumatic Encephalopathy) and untreated brain concussions. I discovered potential treatments that can reverse the symptoms, so to get more information, I made an appointment with a neurological chiropractor just minutes from Bruce's new "home." After meeting with the doctor, he concludes there's a chance he could help us; however, the treatment will cost about $10,000.00, and it isn't covered by Bruce's insurance.

It was worth a try, so after getting an agreement from Bruce that he would cooperate and telling him we would need to raise the money for the treatment, we decided to go for it. If we didn't try, I would regret it, and I would always play the "what if" scenario as a broken record in my mind.

So Mom and I started baking, and with baked goods in my car, I went door-to-door to businesses doing what I call a traveling bake sale. I shared Bruce's story with folks, and in five or six bake sales, we had all the money for the treatment.

I tell the fundraising part of the story not to brag but to express I was willing to go to any lengths and take any avenue that would lead to a potential recovery. We did the bake sales with high hopes that Bruce could eventually return to a typical or semi-normal life, not have to be in a facility, and regain his short-term memory.

Long story short, the doctor saw some progress, but to take things to the next level, there were things that Bruce needed to do to help the process along. Though he had agreed to cooperate before the fundraising and the start of treatments, he faltered, and the treatments stopped. The disease continued to progress, and things worsened.

After about six months of Bruce getting settled in, Bruce's attitude of being at the assisted living facility turns super negative. Things go south between us relationship-wise. He no longer wanted me to take him to any of his doctor appointments and refused visits from Mom and me. He sees me as the one who took everything away from him. I understand that part of this anger can come from the disease. However, we found out that his main friend and former neighbor would call him daily, sometimes several times a day, and badmouth Mom and me. We assume it's because we didn't give him what he wanted of Bruce's items when we did yard sales before putting Bruce's house on the market. I'm angry that this is all happening, and knowing the possible course that this disease will take my brother is disappointing.

Even though there's nothing I can do to change things, my heart hurt that my brother had such hatred towards me. My enthusiasm for life in general, took a nose dive. I started waking up with such dread that another day had been given to me on this earth.

When people would ask me how I was doing, I would smile and say, "Fine." For nine months, I woke up with the dread of another day, hoping that feeling would go away. My Mom started seeing a little less of my joyful self and this unhappy daughter walking around like I had lost something super valuable. And, in all honesty, I had.

Out of all three of my brothers, Bruce was the one I was closest to. I only did what needed to be done for his well-being. It gave me no pleasure to move him away from his house, where he had one or two friends that he hung out with. I didn't take any joy in placing him into an assisted living facility where most people were older and in worse shape than him.

After weeks of Bruce's outbursts against me were filled with feelings of hatred and his refusing visits, the load of rejection and hurt I was carrying became unbearable. The overwhelming dread had become my constant companion as I processed the loss of my brother's trust and friendship. I couldn't take it anymore and finally went to a couple in my church family. I proceeded to tell them what was taking place in my life and that despite my times of prayer, Bible reading, and worship time, I was drowning. I was drowning in dread and couldn't do life like this anymore.

I hadn't cried in quite some time. I was numb. As I shared what was happening, I broke down in uncontrollable sobs. The couple prayed with me and for me, agreeing that I couldn't do this anymore and needed God's strength. I needed Him to live through me, and I felt some of the weight I had been carrying get a little lighter.

For months that followed, I continued to wake up with dread. Even though I had asked God to help me before, I started asking with anticipation that things would eventually be different.

The dread of each morning didn't go away all at once. It seemed to gradually diminish each day until one morning, it was gone. My brother still won't take any of my calls and often communicates his hatred towards me to our other sibling, but I cannot be weighted down with something I can't control. There are some things in life you have to choose to just let go and this was one of them.

I can continue to pray for him, and when the dread or despair tries to steal the joy of my salvation, I can cast down every imagination that is high and exalted against the knowledge of God and bring into captivity every thought to the obedience of Christ.[25] And I like what Jesus' half-brother James wrote that tells us that we can submit ourselves to God, resist our enemy, the devil, and our enemy has to leave us.[26] Every area of our life, including our thoughts, is to be towards God. We show our love to God when we yield ourselves to Him, which positions us to receive His love more fully.

That's What Love Looks Like. #Carefree!

CHAPTER 32

I am NOT Going to Help!

After almost a year of Bruce being in the assisted living facility, I received a phone call I didn't want to believe. I was told that our brother was coming to pick Bruce up and take him home to live with him in Georgia.

This decision would have major impacts. Bruce would lose all his healthcare benefits by taking him out of the facility, and moving him out of state would have other ramifications. All the work done to get him the care he received would go down the drain. There were loads of other things that were my concern in Bruce being taken out-of-state, but they aren't significant to this story.

To say I lost it and was livid is putting it mildly. I was red hot mad and called our brother. Unless a miracle healing occurred, things would worsen as the disease progresses. Eventually, I would be called on to arrange a facility placement when things became unmanageable. After confirming that the news of the move was correct, I hung up the phone with my brother, and out loud, with much emotion, I declared, "I am NOT going to help when the other shoe drops. I'm just not!!" And very quietly,

God's Spirit said, "Really?" It was wrong for me to think this way, so I made the decision to help if and when assistance was needed.

Six months later, I got "THE" phone call. Bruce was getting combative, and our brother thought he needed to be readmitted to a facility. But something magical happened and proved to me that *this is what love looks like,* and I was seeing it active in ME! Wowee!!

The first thing that my brother Craig said was he was sorry that he hadn't listened to the advice that Mom and I offered about not moving Bruce. He admitted that the move was a mistake. And even though I was aware that his motives for arranging the move weren't all that great, I started to cry. I remember focusing on my brother Craig's giving, gentle, and loving heart. He has always been the type of person helping someone else, even if it was an inconvenience to himself. I had always admired that about Craig, though many would take advantage of him through the years for that exact reason. I remember telling him, "I know you did it because you love our brother and thought you were doing what was best for Bruce." I also remember telling him that he didn't need to keep apologizing as he was saying sorry several times. I continued to cry and feel such deep love for Craig I had never experienced before or since in over sixty years. It was an unimaginable experience.

Love truly doesn't keep a record of wrongs others do to us, and love actually covers wrong-doings.[27] That's incredibly powerful to me.

That's What Love Looks Like. #MERCIFUL!

CHAPTER 33

Is it Time Yet?

It's been over six years since I left the food pantry job, and several times during those years, I had considered getting a part-time job. However, each time I looked at job openings, I felt a hesitancy to wait. I had learned my lesson before about taking a job at the wrong time, so I wouldn't do a rewind and repeat! No spider bites or heart blockages for me, thank you! I didn't want a new target on my back for the enemy of my soul to use as his dart board. I was struggling emotionally and had just come out of a very dark place after a few years of waking up with dread. The dreadful clouds had lifted, and I felt drawn to and released in returning to the workforce.

So, in 2019, I put my resume on several websites and interviewed at a local appliance store. I was offered the job during the interview. I accepted the position on a Tuesday and was to start the following Monday. It would be in a field I wasn't familiar with, but I felt comfortable that I could perform the clerical tasks with on-the-job training. Two days after accepting this job, I received a call from one of the elders at the local church I was attending, and they were looking for someone to work in the church office. They had prayed about who to offer the job to, and my name continued to surface. I met with the elder-of-elders to discuss the details and told him I would pray. A couple of hours later, I accepted the church offer, called the appliance store, and told them of the change.

Looking back, I can see how God prepared me for this job. It blows my mind that all the skill sets and the personality I've developed from childhood have contributed to and complement what I do today. I LOVE my job (except for the matching of receipts to credit card statements) because I get to participate in seeing God move in the lives of others. And did I mention that not only would the starting pay be two dollars more an hour than the appliance job but my hours would be flexible? I'm so thankful that my Mom could witness a bounce back into my step as the job brought much joy and purpose into my life.

This is What Love Looks Like. #PREPARATION!

CHAPTER 34

Prepared for Less Grace?!?

It's been just over a year since my Dad passed away, and with my Mom being 90 years old, the obvious of me outliving my Mom was probable. With all we had been through together, including caring for my Dad and dealing with my brother's condition, I wasn't in shape spiritually or mentally to have a life without my Mom being beside me.

My bond with my Mom was a beautiful thing. We could talk about anything, and we were there for one another. She was my best friend, and we talked every day, sometimes several times a day. We laughed, and we cried together. We celebrated with one another, prayed together, and read God's Word together. And for about six years, I would spend two or three days and nights with her each week. I estimate we had over 6,000 phone calls in the past eight years of her life. I'd join her as she volunteered weekly at a local food pantry. And even though she barely won, we'd play her favorite game, Scrabble, several times a day.

This poem was written and given to her in 2003 when I had a heavy traveling schedule, and she was suffering with some health challenges. By the way, my Mom's first name is Grace.

"I Love You More" By DiLeigh Grace:

I love you more than words can tell.
It springs within me as in a well.

The times together have been so few.
It seems like yesterday I was just two.

Over the years, you've become so dear,
and in my heart, I'll hold you near.

You've been a great mom and my best friend,
but best of all I'll see you again.

It's not because you or I are so great,
but because of Jesus' love called GRACE!

As beautiful as this relationship was, my dependency on my Mom needed to decrease and shifted towards the Lord. I even talked to her about this struggle. We often expressed how much we loved our time together and how much we appreciated what we did for one another, and I started praying about this. I felt like I needed to resolve this massive unreadiness of losing her.

That was in the fall of 2018, a few months after my Dad passed away, and in February or March 2019, I felt a peace and a settling in my spirit. And though she didn't have any significant health issues (still driving at age 90), I shared how

God was doing a deep work in me, and when her time came to be with Him, I would be okay. I wanted her to know God was answering prayer. I didn't realize then that it would be sooner than later that I'd find out how prepared I was.

My Mom's life was an expression of *What Love Looks Like.*
#GRACE-FULL!

CHAPTER 35

Why Didn't I Stay?!?

My Mom was put on a prescription to help her with a skin condition that she'd suffered with most of her adult life. Unfortunately, many prescription side affects contributed to her demise. In less than three months, she had a bad fall, a heart attack in her sleep, and a stroke. She lost her ability to speak and swallow. She didn't want a feeding tube, so we granted her wishes to let her go and to make her comfortable.

The last week of her life, she was in the hospital with hospice care, and I visited her daily, but only for a few minutes at a time. After almost three months of caring for her alongside hospital staff, I needed extra rest. She was comatose, and I guess my brief visits were a way of protecting myself from the pain of seeing her suffer.

On July 15, 2019, I stayed several hours. Before I left that night, I told her it was okay for her to "go home" and that one of her grandsons wouldn't be able to come for a visit due to another death in his in-laws' family. All the other grandchildren and my brother Craig had visited, and I felt she may have been waiting for the one grandchild to arrive. I told her how much I loved her and assured her I would be okay. I promised her I would keep my eyes on Jesus and see her again soon.

Two hours later, she passed away, the one time I would have loved for her to NOT do what I had told her to do! There was no doubt in her mind that she was loved much, but if I could do it over, I would have stayed with her until her last breath was breathed. These thoughts stayed with me and ended up in this poem on 9/22/2019.

"Why Didn't I Stay?" By DiLeigh Grace:

I really need to get some things off my chest,
for I find myself not in a place of rest.
I keep asking myself why did I go and not stay,
beside my Mom as she left to go on her way.

Just hours before I had spoken to her beside her bed.
Telling her not to be troubled or worry her little head.
That we would be alright and it was okay to leave.
I didn't want her to suffer anymore; she needed relief.

Today I asked, "Why, Lord, did you not prompt me to stay?!
I would have listened and have been quick to obey!"
I know You were there with her when she left to be forever with You,
but I wish I could have been with her, to see the journey through.

The last few days of her life, it seemed like I just detached from her.
I believe now it was my way of saying to her,
don't delay, that's what I concur.

I need to remind myself I was there for Mom.
When she needed me the most, I didn't leave my post.

I kept telling her how much I loved her, but I gave her some space.
And now it's really time to stop this blame
game and give myself some grace.

Don't forget, I say to myself. This isn't all there is.
One day soon you'll experience eternal bliss.

In the meantime, Mom wouldn't want you to live in regret.
It will stifle your growth and cause you to forget.

In the laughter and the fun times, we loved one another much.
And that's the honest-to-God truth, and I have to focus on such.

So I wrap up this reflection time with a prayer,
"God, help me go through this grief process with less wear and tear!

I know You are Faithful, and I know You are True.
I know You're near me when I'm feeling the blues.

Thank you, Lord, for healing my heart.
A little at a time, part by part.

I know it's a process I need to go through,
and eventually, it won't hurt as bad as my love continues to grow for You."

That's What Love Looks Like. #ASSURANCE!

CHAPTER 36

Continued Grace in the Grief

The following poem was written on the plane ride back home on 10/19/19 after spending some time with my Mom's family and scattering her ashes where we had previously scattered my brother's and Dad's ashes the year before.

I'm heading back home from Connecticut.
Some chapters of life have ended, have shut.
We celebrated Mom's life and had some laughs.
We looked at pictures and shared some gaffs.

I realize now that you're not coming back,
but our God says, I will not lack.
I'll not lack in joy, in peace, or love,
because the Holy Spirit has descended on me like a dove.

Some days, I feel like I'm in a bad dream,
and I'll wake up, and you will ask for some ice cream.
I believe things will improve with time,
as I learn to trust Jesus more and more with my life.

He's a faithful God, and He's really the best-est.
He'll cradle and rock me like a mother in His rest.
Yesterday's gone, and I need to focus on today.
I can only do that as I continue to pray.

Even in sorrow, grief, and pain,
there's joy unspeakable; there's much to gain.
Because Your love and peace are so real,
this is truth, and it doesn't matter how I feel.

You're a faithful God, and You make life complete,
as people learn of You and worship at Your feet.
It's so easy to not have compassion for others,
as cares of life try to steal and smother.

But You live inside of me; this I can't hide.
People so need You, Lord, this I can't deny.
I hate being selfish and keeping to myself.
I don't want to be like an old book, dusty on a shelf.

God, please mold me on the Potter's wheel,
so others will know You and to You they will kneel.

Reading this poem on 9/29/22 for the first time in years,
I can see how God has provided comfort and rest in His
presence. He is so faithful, patient, loving, and kind.

That's What Love Looks Like. #ANTICIPATION!

Love in Action

Acts of Kindness, Paying Love Forward, & The Transformative Power of Love

CHAPTER 37

Why Can't I Just Get To Bed Early?

It's January 2021, and I've just become a dog owner after not having a dog for over 20 years. I was having a hard time coping with the loss of my Mom and thought getting a rescue dog would bring some added joy and companionship. It's been wonderful having my Lola, a Corgie/Chihuahua mix. I believe she rescued me!

Within 24 hours, Lola had become very attached to me, and in less than a few months, we became inseparable. She goes with me everywhere except to worship services or meetings I attend a few times a month.

It was about that time when I had a bizarre dream. In the dream, a man was in bed with a dog on the bed. The dog was very loving towards him even though the assumed owner broke the dog's leg. I could sense the dog's pain, and even though it was being injured, it was forgiving and went back to the owner. In the dream, the owner broke another of the dog's legs. Around the time the dream got to the dog having a third leg broken, I awoke and was in tears. My heart was hurting from what I witnessed, even though I realized moments later it wasn't real.

At first, I didn't understand why I had had the dream. I hadn't eaten anything strange or watched any bad news before bedtime. I don't watch violent movies, read any violent material, or play any video games that would have a combative bent to them. I don't even have a television hookup to any stations! Why did I have the dream and what did it mean? I couldn't shake the sadness and trauma I witnessed in my sleep and thought there might be something I needed to learn from it.

I have had trouble getting to bed at a decent hour for several years. When I say "decent," I mean before midnight; most days, it would be between 2 a.m. and 5 a.m. before I head to the bedroom. For the longest time, I thought it was due to dissatisfaction with how many things I would accomplish in a day. I just wanted to get one more thing done before getting to sleep. I even attributed the problem to working the night shift for almost seven years in my late teens and early twenties and working long hours for decades. And though these things may contribute to the problem, I had a hunch that there was something else, so for years, I prayed for understanding. I hated feeling like a Mack truck had hit me when I would wake up a few hours later to start a new day, but it wouldn't be enough to change my habit and get to bed earlier. I got my answer a few hours after I awoke from the dream.

God showed me that I would avoid going to the bedroom at night because of the abuse I had endured for several years in the evening in my marriage bed with husband #2. The dog represented me, and my husband, who abused me for years, was the dog owner. In real life, I was like the dog in the dream, forgiving and continuing to return to him even though the abuse continued.

I've only shared this dream with two or three close friends. Hopefully sharing it here will help someone else to know that if you don't understand something you're struggling with, ask God for the answers. He loves His children and will reveal things to them in His timing. We often don't have because we don't ask,[28] and if we lack wisdom, we can ask Him for it, and He will give it to us.[29]

Even though it was hard to see what was occurring in the dream, it allowed me to put my finger on the root cause of the problem to overcome it. Until this was revealed to me, I had no idea that the abuse I had experienced was the very thing that was causing me to stay up late at night.

I haven't conquered this situation, but since understanding the dream, I've made progress in having more days than not in getting to bed earlier. That relationship is no longer part of my life; I am safe now. There is no reason to fear that my bedroom is a place of torment or mistreatment. It's now a place of refuge and welcomes me.

That's What Love Looks Like. #SOLUTIONS!

CHAPTER 38

Bye, Bye Paradise!

It's March 2021, and a friend of mine by the name of Jenny has desperately needed a house. She, like I, loves that place I call paradise. So I started looking to find a place for her.

I found a place in the same county, 30 minutes from my apartment, but it's not what she wants. Before I know it, I'm buying the place. It's not like I was buying an outfit or clueless while making the purchase, but I wasn't looking to buy a property that day! I was buying 2/3 of an acre of land and a home built less than two years prior. It was in a nice neighborhood, and because it is at the end of a cul-de-sac, very little traffic comes down the street, so it's nice and quiet.

On May 1, 2021, I wrote the following poem in honor of my Dad.

"Moving Along" By DiLeigh Grace:

Three years ago today Dad,
you went to your final resting place.
A part of me went with you even though I'm in a different space.

You'd be happy to hear I'm moving again soon,
to a place where I can see many stars and gaze up at the moon.

There are fruit trees and lots of grass to mow.
And I want to plant a garden, there's lots for me to learn and know.

I don't have Mom's green thumb, but my Heavenly Father knows it all.
I will draw closer to Him, and on His Word I'll stand tall.

I'm looking forward to making my final move,
to my heavenly home, where all is wonderfully smooth.

You quickly left this earth when I stepped away from your side;
but we'll be together forever, for we are part of Christ's bride.

You are my Dad, I am your daughter. Love you loads, Dad!

The apartment rent had more than doubled in the three and a half years I had lived there, and I would eventually need to move. Even though it wasn't something I intended to do so soon, I had gotten into a mundane, coasting-like state of living. It was a great time to make the change.

I was counter-offered on the initial purchase price I made. I called a friend who would help me pray on what to offer, and while we were on the phone, the Lord gave her a figure I should counter-offer back with. So I called my Realtor and told him a dollar amount of $ 5,000.00 more than my friend advised. My offer was given based on fear.

There's still a housing shortage in this area of Florida; other people were looking at the place, and I didn't want to lose the contract. As soon as I hung up with my Realtor, the Lord spoke to me and said, "That's not what I told you to do." Seconds later, I called back my Realtor as he was immediately going to communicate the higher price to the seller and told him, "Don't send that amount I just gave you!!" I told him to offer $5,000.00 less. The seller agreed to the price that my friend advised me to give.

That's What Love Looks Like. #DIVINE*DIRECTION!

CHAPTER 39

From Paradise to MoUrning to Morning

I still see my church family I've been with for over 10 years, but being 30 minutes away, I feel disconnected. I've been struggling with bouts of aloneness for quite some time. Even before moving, I was dealing with this. I don't know if this makes sense to you, but it's not loneliness I feel but aloneness. And the feeling of aloneness at times is almost deafening. It's just too quiet.

I love all the things I'm involved with: my involvement with two church families, my part-time job as an administrator, playing the piano, writing songs, and singing, the ladies' Bible study I teach bi-weekly, a senior's group I have lunch with monthly, bingo, and praying with people I meet in the marketplace. Sounds like my life is pretty full, but it's different than having someone close to me I can share my life with or pick up the phone any time of the day or night and say, "Guess what just happened!"

I'm not writing this so you can feel sorry for me. Sometimes, I appreciate living alone; if I want to delay washing the dishes or putting something away, no problem. I'm the only one who will give myself a hard time about it unless I hear a familiar saying of my Mom's tease my mind, saying, "Put it away, not down!"

I have a few friends who would drop everything to help me should I ever need their help. I'm very grateful for them. They even include me in festivities during holidays or for Sunday dinners. Still, they have families and responsibilities of their own whereas I don't. Other than my dog, it's just me. The feeling of aloneness has been heavy on me for quite some time. My mornings were getting more challenging, for I would wake up with the thought of another day of the same. It was heading in the direction of dread I had experienced years before.

One day I was talking to a mentor of mine and sharing this dreariness with him. Suddenly, I felt this overwhelming presence of God flood me. God said that He wanted to change my mourning to mornings! He showed me right then that there was just one letter difference between the two words. They sound identical but what a difference with the one little letter of u! Then, the Lord spoke to my heart and mind, saying, "If you stop focusing on yoU when you wake up in the morning and turn your focus towards me, you will see a change take place!" Joy hit me, and I was so thankful for this encounter and encouragement from the Lord. *That's what love looks like!* He cares enough about me to speak into any situation of my life that's a concern or a hindrance to my living an abundant life.

I'm still working on this refocusing thing. My mornings are better now, and I would say 90% of the time, I wake up with either lyrics to a specific worship song or a Bible verse fresh on my mind. I then intentionally think about those words and start praying as I begin a new day. That's so much better than thinking about me, myself, and I. Though the amount of time alone hasn't changed, my focus has turned toward the One that says, "He'll never leave me or forsake me,[30] and He will be with me always, in every circumstance, forever.[31]

Though I know He's with me all the time, I still pray that God will provide me with a close friend or two (with skin on) that I can share life with, do ministry beside, and, if need be, have a conversation in the middle of the night because....

....I believe *That's What Love Looks Like. #SHARING*LIFE!*

CHAPTER 40

Thriving Not Just Surviving

It's August 2022, and I found this poem I had written on 4/6/22, which I am finishing as I type this chapter. Much has happened since I penned the first half of it. I was dissatisfied with my relationship with God because my daily experiences with Him didn't align with my desired personal growth. It's a good thing. This hunger was growing inside of me at a rate I had never experienced in all of my life. A month or two before writing this poem, I had signed up for a Love Encounters Workshop run by a ministry called Live in Your Destiny. In this three to seven-day workshop, I learned basic yet essential principles of receiving God's love from my head to my heart and experiencing that love in tangible ways. Never before had I heard the scriptures presented in the practical and applicable ways shared in this workshop. It blew my mind and changed my heart. A week after I wrote this poem, I made a 12-week commitment with this same ministry to be more intentional with the journey I wanted to take. Though it was a financial sacrifice to do so, I signed up for the Love Encounters LIFESTYLE workshop. There were other commitments that I had to agree with that would involve a minimum of ten hours a week of individual and group activities. It was a big deal, as is encountering the living God!

I can't say every day is a breeze, but I'm more connected to my Father in heaven than ever. I'm also more aware that I'm not doing this life alone. Every concern and every joy is something He wants me to share with Him. In the second half of this poem, I've tried to express what the past 12 weeks have turned into: a lifestyle of communing with the Lord throughout the day.

This quote from C.S. Lewis in his work titled To Love is to be Vulnerable, can sometimes explain how we respond to loss-related challenges: "If you love deeply, you're going to hurt deeply. But it's still worth it." I couldn't agree more!

"Now that You're Gone" By DiLeigh Grace:

Since you've been gone Mom, it's been so hard.
But I'm intentionally seeking our great Lord.

I'm glad you're not here, here to see,
all the recent news and calamities.

I wish I could talk to you every day.
There are so many things I'd like to say.

Our God has been Faithful, True, and Kind.
Daily He's changing me, renewing my mind.

I'm learning to dwell on things I cannot see.
And live a life more full and free.

I've met a group called Live in Your Destiny.
Having a heart connection with God is their specialty.

They're teaching me to open up my heart,
telling God what I'm feeling is a great start.

But feelings can be misleading,
for they camouflage what we're really needing.

I thought I was done with the grieving process,
but then, one morning, I was one hot mess.

I woke up one day angry and frustrated.
The feelings I had were very weighted.

I told the Lord, "I'm angry, I'm frustrated, and I don't know why!
Would you show me and help me see things through your eyes?"

He then brought to memory of a time when I was with you.
It was something funny and then I needed some tissues.

I laughed and then I cried for almost an hour.
I felt His presence as He is my strong tower.

The anger and frustration may have been what I was feeling
but my need from Him was comfort, safety, and healing.

I'm learning to trust Him more and more.
Most days it's easy and less of a chore.

Nowadays, I awake with a song, a pleasant memory, or a Bible verse.
Different from the recent past when things seem to be going from bad to worse.

Just days after writing the above poem, I received a text from my former (sounds better than ex) sister-in-law from my first marriage asking me if I'd like to attend their family reunion. Other than seeing them briefly at my #1 husband's funeral five years prior, I had not seen most of the family for 24 years. With me praying about the need for connectivity with family, this text was such a great surprise. Seeing everyone again for a day of catching up and good food was super special!

Between the Lord giving me clarity on why I was feeling angry and frustrated to reconnecting with some family members I'd been missing over the years, I am again reminded that....

....That's What Love Looks Like. #RELATIONSHIPS!

CHAPTER 41

A New Song

Fast forwarding to today – 2022. I'm working on finishing this book (yeah, it's been slllloooow!), and here is my journal entry I made on 7/11/22:

Before heading to bed, I watched my Mom's home-going service and doing much reminiscing about her and Dad. I then went outside for a few minutes to let my dog out, and the stillness of the night was terrific. Looking up into the sky, the moon was shining brightly through the clouds and the shape of the light resembled a silhouette of the face of Jesus. I spoke to my heavenly Father and declared the truth of His existence and the longing I had in my heart to see Him. I verbally renounced all doubt that He was a fairy tale and that this life was all there is, and then I retired for the night.

This morning, I awoke to new words and a melody. The words were: "Let my life be an offering. Everything, all of me, I bring". I kept singing these two lines because I didn't want to lose what was being downloaded into my head and heart. I got up, went to my piano, and put the rest of the song together. On the way to the piano, I realized today is 7/11, my earthly father's birthday.

What a gift that my heavenly Dad gave me and a great way to start the day! My moUrnings are becoming less frequent, and I am beginning to have God-centered mornings!

It's been a fascinating journey, and God continues to show His faithfulness, especially when I haven't been faithful. The struggle is real, but He's still giving me songs, and I am determined to finish this book.

That's What Love Looks Like. STEADY!

CHAPTER 42

Do You Live in a Barn?

This incident happened in the 1980s. Though it's not chronological like the other chapters in this book, it's another example worth sharing of God's ability to change a person willing to be changed.

Sad to say, the title of this chapter is the very words I spoke once to my mother-in-law. Unfortunately, I was a very frustrated, young, married woman who blamed my mother-in-law for all the flaws I saw in my husband. This is so wrong, but the story gets better as you read further.

My in-laws just arrived, and my mother-in-law constantly left the front door open. The air conditioning was on, and I'm sure there was a call from within to invite all the mosquitoes and every other flying creature into the house. If you've ever been to Florida, you know there are all kinds of creeping things that love our warm weather. They belong outside. In the woods. Or in a barn. And not inside the house!

So I yelled to my mother-in-law, "Shut the front door! Do you live in a barn??" Not only did everyone in my house hear me shouting, but I think the neighborhood clearly understood what was happening and that I wanted the front door shut.

I didn't have a stopwatch, but it had to be within five minutes when I heard a voice speak to my heart. This voice was the opposite of my loud and impatient outburst but just as audible, if not more so. Oh, yeah! I'm sure no one else could hear it, but I heard it. I heard HIM, and what He had to say to me, He didn't have to repeat twice! He very lovingly told me I couldn't claim to belong to Him and treat my mother-in-law the way I was treating her.

God loved me enough to let me know in that moment that I couldn't wear His label and be clothed with His name on my life while speaking hatefully to others. So I told Him how sorry I was, then apologized to my mother-in-law.

I don't recall whether I apologized in front of the other family members or just to my mom-in-law, but God continued to do a work in my heart. He continued showing me how my ugly thoughts manifested in not-so-pretty behaviors. Shortly after that, my sister-in-law, who was at my house at the time of the incident just weeks before, came to me and asked me, "What has happened to you? You're not the same person you were weeks and even years before!"

If anyone boasts, "I love God," and goes right on hating his brother or sister, thinking nothing of it, he is a liar. If he won't love the person he can see, how can he love the God he can't see?[32] Loving God includes loving people. This is how others will know that we are disciples of Jesus. When they see the love we have for others.[33] Those are strong words, but I like it when someone communicates in a straightforward style that leaves little room for misinterpretation.

All the glory goes to God for this transformation only He can bring about when a person repents and asks for forgiveness.

Now *That's What Love Looks Like. #CORRECTION!*

CHAPTER 43

Mountain, Music Equipment, & White Flower

I've shared how I've experienced God's love in messy, uncomfortable, demanding, sad, complex, and disappointing situations. His love is real to me! I've expressed how God's love has flowed into me, and now I want to share a few brief stories of how His love has flowed out of me. I have dozens of stories like these, but here are just a few. This is to honor the One that is so deserving.

I often pray for people in the marketplace, in a chat session, or on the phone. I find it exciting to see how God will show up when we simply ask someone, "Is there something I can pray with or for you about today?" Some respond with seconds of total silence, some with warm expressions of surprise that they would be asked such a question, while very few may say, "No, thank you, I'm good!"

It's around the year 2008, and I'm in the Atlanta airport getting a meal at one of the sit-down restaurants, and I get a male server who I'll call Daniel. After he takes my food order, I ask God if He wants me to share anything specific with Daniel. I then visualize a basement with lots of musical instruments. As I started conversing with Daniel, I told him that sometimes God shows me things to share with others and wondered if he had a basement of musical instruments. His eyes got large and confirmed what I shared with him. I told him that God had given him the talent and love for music. I also told him God wanted him to use those abilities to bring people to know Him and that if he asked for direction, God would bless him and his efforts. How good is God that He would take time to assure Daniel that his love for music was something He intentionally placed inside him and could be a career change?

It's 10/10/22, and I called a website development company, and a gal named Dayah took my call. At the end of our conversation, I asked her if I could pray with her about anything. She told me that her Mom, who has diabetes, needed prayer. After I prayed, she told me she didn't understand what was happening to her, but she was crying. I told her a mountain appeared in my mind while praying. I asked her if mountains had any particular significance to her. She told me she had a mountain tattoo and, again, she didn't understand what she was feeling. I assured her that she was experiencing the love of her Father and that He was inviting her to have a relationship with Him. I also shared how God had healed me of diabetes as a youth and that a price had already been paid for her Mother's healing. God would heal her Mom, and He was to get all the credit for the miracle. The conversation ended with her saying that she was taking her break time to pray. What a delight it was to talk with Dayah!

I'll never forget a conversation I had with a gal on 8/5/22. I made this journal entry that afternoon: There's rejoicing going on in heaven right now and in my living room! I had to make a phone call to a bank, and Tatiana took my call. After getting permission to pray for Tatiana, I began praying, and she interrupted me, saying she was feeling a presence. I explained to her who it was that she felt. While praying for her, a picture of a white flower became my focus. So I asked her if a white flower meant anything to her, and she started laughing. She told me she was drinking from a cup with a white flower. I had previously mentioned that God knows her and knows everything about her. I obviously wouldn't have known she had a white-flowered cup, but the One who loves her lives inside me and knows everything. Out of all the people in the world that He loves, He wanted her to know at that moment that He was interested in her specifically. Typically, I would have wrapped up the conversation. Instead, I gave her a few more examples of God encounters with other people I had had. She was engaged and seriously interested in what I was sharing, so I asked her if she wanted to know this Jesus I'd been talking about. After saying yes, we prayed together which included her inviting Jesus into her life and for Him to take complete control. I asked the Holy Spirit to fill her to overflowing with His presence, and then she gave me confirmation of her new birth.

What a great way to live day-to-day! Time is short, and from now on, I will ask God to use me more in speaking into the lives of those I get the privilege of meeting, whether in person or at a distance. I want everyone to experience His presence and love, one person at a time.

Thank you, God, for Your Holy Spirit that gives us the POWER to be salt and light and for allowing us to share hope and life with others; it's up close and personal.

That's What Love Looks Like. INTIMATE!

CHAPTER 44

The Million Dollar Question

When God first impressed upon me to write this book, a conversation came to my mind that was between His Son and an expert teacher of the law who studied and copied the Hebrew scriptures. The Law was the teachings of God that the people had prior to Jesus' time on the earth. This conversation occurred after Jesus had answered several questions from those trying to trip him up and bring confusion to His followers. The question asked was a very important one. The conversation is noted in several places in the Bible.[34] Here is how the dialogue goes per The Voice translation in the writings of Mark.[35]

Scribe: Tell me, Teacher. What is the most important thing that God commands in the law?

Jesus: The most important commandment is this: "Hear, O Israel, the Eternal One is our God, and the Eternal One is the only God. You should love the Eternal, your God, with all your heart, with all your soul, with all your mind, and with all your strength." The second great commandment is this: "Love others in the same way you love yourself." There are no commandments more important than these.

Scribe: You have spoken the truth. For there is one God and only one God, and to love God with all our heart and soul and mind and strength and to love our neighbors as ourselves are more important than any burnt offering or sacrifice *we* could ever give.

Jesus heard that the man had spoken with wisdom.

Jesus: Well said; if you understand that, then the kingdom of God is closer than you think.

Though Jesus is asked what is the most important commandment, notice Jesus' response includes naming not just one commandment but two commandments. As The Voice translation points out, these two commandments cannot be separated. If you love like Jesus is speaking of here, we cannot love God and ignore those around us.

Here's my takeaways of Jesus' words:

1. He is defining to Israel (and all of mankind) that the One that desires to be loved above all others and above everything else is THE Eternal One and that He is the ONLY God. I have read this scripture dozens of times and never noticed this portion of the conversation. So good! Jesus is giving credibility to the words He spoke then and to those of us reading it centuries later. Jesus always spoke things in union with His Father's heart and what He heard the Father say.[36] That would make what Jesus said way more important than words spoken by me or anyone else on the planet! So whenever we hear

quotes of Jesus, they are important enough to pay close attention to.

2. The most significant thing mankind (all men— not gender specific) can do is to love this Eternal God—through a personal relationship with Him— withholding nothing. Loving Him with EVERY THING that makes us who we are. Loving Him with ALL our heart, soul, mind, and strength.

3. Love others in the same manner we love ourselves.

4. The understanding that the law student had received was from the heavenly realm and was a far different way of thinking than what would come out of an earthly kingdom. The earthly kingdom's mindset is to put yourself first regardless of the harm or disadvantage it would bring to others.

I'm reminded of a child's game that we played called Barrel of Monkeys. We dumped the plastic monkeys out of the barrel onto the table. We would start the game by picking up a monkey on the table by the arm and then hooking the first monkey's other arm into the second monkey's arm. We would continue this process by making a chain of monkeys. The object of the game was to connect all the monkeys before dropping any of them.

Thinking back to these two commandments, think of the first monkey as the "love your God" and then the second one as "love others." Without these two being linked together at the start, life will have a very different outcome. It's God's pleasure that we have a life full of His love and love for others. Without these two commandments being our heartbeat, godly principles cannot be picked up, linked, or put into their rightful place in our lives. Everything good in our lives and to be experienced depends on these two truths.[37]

We can't trust our own hearts, our soulish desires, or our minds if we think and live with the opinions and ideals of a world that does not know Him. Our nature is to hide our weaknesses or behave like they don't exist. That is not the will of God in our lives. In writing this book, I had to look in the rearview mirror, and in doing so, I am reminded of *What Love Looks Like*. Sounds simple, and it is, but it's not always easy! Does it sometimes seem impossible to you? I'm glad that God is drawn to those who admit they are powerless, and then He fills them with His power!

I never felt so weak when there was little I could do when my Mom fell in my arms the night she put my Dad and her best friend into the first nursing home. BUT God came through, and the grief I experienced was lifted. My weakness was very evident when I wasn't sure where I would live or whether I would end up divorced a second time when Claus offered me a silver platter, BUT God my Father had already given me everything I will ever need in giving me His Son. I was so drained and weak as I walked that beach after going through the second divorce and feeling all so alone. For over a year after leaving my second husband, I had spent hours speechless and sobbing in prayer when, in His presence, I found strength. God pouring the oil of joy into my very being after months of discontentment with living in the "dog choir" house was priceless. And the overwhelming love of God that flooded by heart for my brother Craig was super-natural.

When we find ourselves in trouble, we can run to Him as our strength, our hiding place, and an immediate help.[38] To those with no strength at all, He increases strength and gives power to the faint.[39] When our soul is weary in sorrow, we can go to His Word where we will find strength.[40] Our strength is made new over and over again when we hope in the Lord, and as a result, we will not get winded or tired; we will not grow weary.[41]

It's been about ten years since the first of several confirmations came about writing this book, and I continue to have experiences that point to my NEED for a Savior. And to the degree that we live these words out depends on whether we are running our own lives or allowing Jesus to be the Lord of our lives and not just the Savior of the world. My greatest desire is to honor God with my life in whatever way He chooses to lead.

IF we are to love God the way He deserves to be loved, we will love Him with every PASSION of our heart, with all the ENERGY of our being, and with every THOUGHT within us. [42] There is no room for anything else. It will cause us to not love something or someone else more than we adore Him. Our time and efforts in this life will all be directed to seeing His kingdom advancing, and our thoughts will be on things that would be on the mind of our Father.

That's where I want to be. It shouldn't be about what WE want for our lives if we are His children. It's about surrendering E-V-E-R-Y T-H-I-N-G to Him and holding on to nothing self-centered or self-seeking. Frequently, we have to retrain our thinking. That's why we must spend time with Him and read His Word where His desires are expressed best. I believe that presenting ourselves to God daily and many times a day allows the Holy Spirit to transform the way we think and to be led by Him.[43] It's only by doing this that He can take our stories and make them something beautiful. It's then we can be imitators of His love and see....

....*That's What Love Looks Like. BEAUTY*

Reflecting on the Journey

Final Words

Embrace Love in Every Chapter of Life

I can't see how I can write about what love looks like without including the most frequently quoted writings that thoroughly define the most powerful force in the world. So here it goes:

If I speak with human eloquence and angelic ecstasy but don't love, I'm nothing but the creaking of a rusty gate.

If I speak God's Word with power, revealing all His mysteries and making everything plain as day, and if I have faith that says to a mountain, "Jump," and it jumps, but I don't love, I'm nothing.

If I give everything I own to the poor and even go to the stake to be burned as a martyr, but I don't love, I've gotten nowhere. So, no matter what I say, what I believe, and what I do, I'm bankrupt without love.

Love never gives up.

Love cares more for others than for self.

Love doesn't want what it doesn't have.

Love doesn't strut,

Doesn't have a swelled head,

Doesn't force itself on others,

Isn't always "me first,"
Doesn't fly off the handle,
Doesn't keep score of the sins of others,
Doesn't revel when others grovel,
Takes pleasure in the flowering of truth,
Puts up with anything,
Trusts God always,
Always looks for the best,
Never looks back,
But keeps going to the end.
Love never dies.
Trust steadily in God, hope unswervingly, love extravagantly.
And the best of the three is love.[44]

If you've read this far, you have learned I've made some bad choices, especially relationship-wise. After my first divorce, getting sexually involved outside of marriage with two guys, with one ending up being my second husband, made me feel unworthy. I sometimes thought I had gone too far for God's forgiveness.

Words of wisdom once penned by C.S. Lewis in The Case for Christianity reads: "Progress means getting nearer to the place you want to be. And if you have taken a wrong turn, then to go forward does not get you any nearer." He continues to say that sometimes you must turn around, pick up where you made the wrong turn, and get on the right road. He then makes the final point that it's in those scenarios that "the man who turns back soonest is the most progressive man." Words of wisdom. We can't go back, but we can realize our mistakes and determine not to continue on a path that will result in an undesirable end.

I love these lyrics that are part of Al Denson's song No Love Lost:

"Change time after time, I seem to let you down
Still, You say it's not too late to turn around
Even after all the things I've done
I could still hear You saying I'm Your precious one
And even though sometimes I don't know why
I realize someday I'll see in Your eyes
There's no love lost"

I recognize that I have hurt the Lord's heart in the past, and it's possible I may make wrong choices in the future, but as He keeps drawing me to Himself, I see this happening less and less. As I spend time with Him daily, it's incredible that He changes me so I look more and more like Him and less like myself, who would otherwise do things my way. He tells me I am worth every drop of blood His Son shed so I can have a close relationship with Him.

I hope that the words you've read on the pages of this book have spoken volumes about the love of a heavenly Father and how His love has been expressed in and through my own life. He's loved me, taught me how to love others, and continues to do this daily.

His love is patient and kind. His love is personal and real, and He wants YOU, His most prized creation, to experience Him. He offers His love through a relationship with His Son, Jesus Christ. If you don't know this love, I encourage you to ask Him to make Himself real to you. I guarantee He will and then receive all He has for you. To continue to position yourself to grow in His love, read

His Word, the Bible. Starting in the gospel of John is an excellent place to read. And reading one chapter a day from Psalm and a chapter a day in the book of Proverbs will give you priceless wisdom and direction that you can apply daily.

That's What Love Looks Like. INVITING!

Notes

1. 1 Corinthians Chapter 13 verse 13
2. Matthew Chapter 22 verses 36-40
3. John Chapter 14 verse 15
4. 1 Samuel Chapter 15 verse 22
5. John Chapter 1 verse 12
6. John Chapter 10 verse 27
7. Psalms Chapter 37 verse 4
8. Job Chapter 23 verse 10
9. Philippians Chapter 2 verse 12
10. Philippians Chapter 4 verse 7
11. John Chapter 10 verse 27
12. Luke Chapter 12 verses 29-32
13. Romans Chapter 14 verse 17
14. Isaiah Chapter 55 verses 8-9
15. Matthew Chapter 7 verse 11
16. Colossians Chapter 3 verse 2
17. Mark Chapter 6 verses 45-54
18. John Chapter 4 verses 1-42
19. Luke Chapter 2 verses 8-20, Matthew Chapter 2 verses 1-11
20. Luke Chapter 2 verses 22-38
21. Proverbs Chapter 15 verse 13

22. Proverbs Chapter 17 verse 22
23. Psalms Chapter 34 verse 18
24. Proverbs Chapter 3 verses 5-6
25. 2 Corinthians Chapter 10 verse 5
26. James Chapter 4 verse 7
27. 1 Corinthians Chapter 13 verse 5 in the Contemporary English Version
28. Matthew Chapter 7 verses 7-8, James Chapter 4 verse 2d
29. James Chapter 1 verse 5
30. Hebrews Chapter 13 verse 5
31. Matthew Chapter 28 verse 20b
32. 1 John Chapter 4 verse 20
33. John Chapter 13 verse 35
34. Matthew Chapter 22 verses 34-40, Mark Chapter 12 verses 28-34, Luke Chapter 10 verses 25-28
35. Mark Chapter 12 verses 28-34
36. John Chapter 12 verse 49
37. Matthew Chapter 22 verse 40
38. Psalms Chapter 46 verse 1
39. Isaiah Chapter 40 verse 29
40. Psalms Chapter 119 verse 28
41. Isaiah Chapter 40 verse 31
42. Matthew Chapter 22 verse 37 in the Passion translation
43. Romans Chapter 12 verses 1-2
44. 1 Corinthians Chapter 13 verses 1-8a,13c in the Message translation

Printed in the United States
by Baker & Taylor Publisher Services

Printed in the United States
by Baker & Taylor Publisher Services